MIND OVER MOJITOS: HOW MODERATING YOUR DRINKING CAN CHANGE YOUR LIFE

EASY RECIPES FOR HAPPIER HOURS & A JOY-FILLED LIFE

CASSANDRA GAISFORD

CONTENTS

Free Workbook! v
Praise for Mind Your Mojitos vii
Author's Note xi

Blame Your Brain? 1
About These Recipes 3
What is Sobriety? 5
You Booze, You Lose 7
Mindful Drinking 9
What Can Sobriety Do? 11
Giving Good Glass 13

PART I

Non-alcoholic Drinks For Spring & Summer 19
1. Virgin Island Fox 20
2. Passion Fruit Bubbly 22
3. Passion Fruit Power Punch 24
4. Mosmo 25
5. H2O Clean & Collected 27
6. Blueberry and Maple Mojito 29
7. Tamarillo Thyme Spritzer 31
8. Virgin Strawberry Daiquiri 33
9. Grapefruit Honey Ginger Soda 35
10. The Meg Ryan: A Bright & Bubbly Blended Berry Drink 37
11. Pineapple Chamomile Tea 39
12. Virgin Mojito 41
13. Raspberry Mint Julep 43
14. Basil Mojito Iced Tea 45
15. Virgin Screwdriver 47
16. Virgin Moscow Mule 49
17. Pre-Mixes & RTD's 52
18. Apple 'No-jito' 55

PART II

Non-alcoholic Drinks for Winter & Fall 59
19. Kiwi Fruit Kiss 60
20. Mulled Cranberry Apple Cider 61
21. Cranberry Fizz Punch 63
22. Spiced Apple Cider 66
23. Hot Mulled Apple Cider & Orange Sangria 68
24. Asian Pear Sparkler 70

A Few Last Words 72
Please Leave A Review 75

EXCERPT: YOUR BEAUTIFUL MIND: CONTROL ALCOHOL

Praise for Your Beautiful Mind 79
The Truths 87
About This Book 89
How to Use This Book 97
Principle One: The Call for Sobriety 103
1. Introduction: The Truth About Sobriety 104
2. Test Your Knowledge 110
3. Alcohol Unmasked 112
4. Savvy Sobriety 120
5. The Surprising Joy of Sobriety 126
6. Problem Drinking? 131
7. Wounded Warriors 142

Also by Cassandra Gaisford 153
Coaching and Wellness Therapies 161
Follow Your Passion to Prosperity Online Course 164

Further Resources 165
Please Leave A Review 171
About the Author 173
Stay In Touch 175
Copyright 177

FREE WORKBOOK!

Thank you for your interest in my new book.

To show my appreciation, I'm excited to be giving you another book for FREE!

Download the free *Find Your Passion Workbook* here: https://worklifesolutions.lpages.co/free-find-your-passion-workbook-control-alcohol

I hope you enjoy it—love is the new drug. This book is dedicated to helping you enjoy sobriety and live and work with passion, resilience and joy.

Passion Workbook

PRAISE FOR MIND YOUR MOJITOS

"Anyone who needs to cut back their drinking, be kept on track or inspired will find genuine help in this honest, insightful book."

~ CS Sloan, counselor

"Fun, simple and just what's needed for a creative break to drinking (that can seriously change your life!)"

~ Russ Perry, author of *The Sober Entrepreneur*

"Cassandra is such a wonderful guide throughout the book to show how sobriety doesn't have to be a prison sentence and it can be fun. I love the sassy and sexy recipes. I also really appreciated her take on the importance of a good glass and that aesthetics are everything when it comes to sobriety and a sexy non-alcoholic beverage that still makes you feel like an adult."

~ Hannah Joy, Health Coach

"Great Writer. Great Recipes. Pleasantly surprised by the quality of writing and the inventiveness of the recipes."

~ Amazon 5-star Review

"More motivating inspiration from Cassandra. Be honest with yourself ... do you drink too much? Do you want to take back the control that alcohol has over you? Cassandra shows you how you can do this without missing out on the fun. Complete abstinence does not have to be the answer, neither does drinking water in boring tumblers at social functions have to be subject to questioning peers.

As the daughter of an alcoholic father, I am well aware of my own predisposition. When he fought for control, he would drink orange juice on ice, in a highball glass with a splash of soda and a wedge of orange. It looked just like a Screwdriver and no-one ever questioned it.

With Cassandra's advice and delicious mocktail recipes, you too can release the grip of alcohol and regain your life."

~ Niki Firth, Amazon Review

"Geared toward problem drinkers struggling to cut back or quit drinking as well as those who want to be reinspired during recovery, this book helps those looking for alternatives to alcohol to take pleasure in booze-free alternatives... For readers who sincerely want to stop drinking the recipes in this book will pave the way."

~ L. Wells, Director

DEDICATION

I dedicate this book to those of you

who are ready to live a beautiful, sober life

This book is also for Lorenzo, my Knight Templar,

who encourages and supports me

to make my dreams possible...

And for all my clients

who have shared their dreams with me,

and allowed me to help them achieve amazing feats.

Thank you for inspiring me.

AUTHOR'S NOTE

"The world is not dangerous because of those who do harm but because of those who look at it without doing anything."

~ Albert Einstein, genius

December 2016—the year I took control of my drinking. Perhaps like you, I'd grown concerned about how much, and how regularly, I was consuming alcohol.

I knew the side-effects, and I didn't like them—insomnia, depression, aggression, muddled thinking, bloating, weight gain and more. But still, I couldn't control alcohol.

One month of sobriety was the longest time I'd ever managed.

I tried reading books, used self-hypnosis, made a star-chart and ticked off my alcohol-free days. There were two ticks one week, none the next, then some longer stretches. But, despite my positive intentions and extraordinary will, booze always reigned victoriously.

Nothing worked.

Until Christmas 2016 when I finally got angry—and scared—enough to make a change. To protect others' privacy I won't go into detail, suffice to say that my turning point involved a rifle, shots fired and fearing for my life.

But my motivation and my personal story of alcohol being in control began earlier than that. My grandmother was an alcoholic. And her father before that—and both their stories, like many people affected by alcohol was one of tragedy.

In the 1930's one drunken brawl outside the local pub in New Zealand left one man dead and my great-grandfather charged with murder.

My grandmother was four, and her brother aged six when they were taken into foster care. They never saw their mother, father or each other again.

Their story, my story, your story is a far too common one.

For many people complete removal of alcohol is the only cure. Western culture does not make it easy—happiness, we are lead to believe, can only be found in a bottle. Changing this mistaken belief is one of the reasons I have written this book.

Mindful drinking

Mind Over Mojitos is not an anti-alcohol book. It offers a fresh approach, encouraging you to view your relationship to alcohol more mindfully and offering you some tasty booze-free alternatives.

While it's important to highlight the dangers of drinking too much, my aim is to highlight the life-changing benefits of drinking far less.

Importantly, I'll share some simple but effective ways to mix, mingle and practice sober socialising—and still feel great.

A fresh approach

Drinking too much is a culturally sanctioned, actively encouraged "cure" for the *dis-ease* of modern life. Except it isn't a cure at all. It's not a sustainable quick fix. Many people are using alcohol, consciously or unconsciously, to self-medicate all or some of the following:

- Stress
- Anxiety
- Depression
- Low self-esteem
- Sexual Abuse
- Trauma
- Shame
- Guilt
- Boredom

There is a cure

Many people who have battled alcohol dependency and addiction overcame obstacles just like you and I. But the single biggest factor was their ability to take control of their drinking.

Sometimes they deferred to experts. Sometimes they turned to God. Sometimes they joined a support group, or they embraced spontaneous sobriety and went it alone.

But the one thing they all had in common was the knowledge that their drinking was taking more than it was giving.

In every instance, when people nailed their drink demons, they universally agreed that their life was more beautiful sober.

"I gave up alcohol in 1980. I enjoyed it far too much, to the point where I frequently got intoxicated. Everything in my life changed for the better stopped. It was the right decision," said the medical doctor and self-empowerment author Deepak Chopra.

Why I wrote this book

The successful pursuit of sobriety is born from my own experience, both professionally as a holistic therapist, and personally as a woman with a genetic predisposition to alcoholism. My desire and determination to liberate others from the clutches of booze inspired this book.

During a recent interview I was asked: 'What do you hope readers get out of *Mind Over Mojitos?* My response was "choice."

If I can help people gain new knowledge, enhance their awareness and fall in love with booze-free alternatives then *Mind Over Mojitos* has made an important and much-needed contribution.

My hope is that *Mind Over Mojito's* easy recipes for happier hours & healthier, joy-filled living will help you achieve your goals—whether that's getting sober or just cutting back—and create positive, permanent transformational change in your life. And that one day, should our paths cross, you will tell me that your life truly is more beautiful sober.

Who Is This Book For?

If you want to control your drinking and live a happier, healthier life on your own terms, this book is for you.

For readers who sincerely want to stop or rescue their drinking, but lack awareness of healthy alcohol-free alternatives, the recipes in this book will pave the way.

If you're a heavy drinker or love someone who is, *Mind Over Mojitos: How Moderating Your Drinking Can Change Your Life* will provide healthy alternatives to drinking alcohol that will empower the journey to wellness and happiness.

Or, you might just want to inspire others and lead the way by controlling alcohol, either by cutting back or giving up completely *Mind Over Mojitos* will come to your rescue.

Mind Over Mojitos: How Moderating Your Drinking Can Change Your Life, will help you:

- Take control of your drinking
- Relieve stress and still have fun
- Enjoy the taste of sexy and healthy alcohol-free alternatives
- Eliminate alcohol to do a life and career reset
- Love drinking minus the booze, hangover, and guilt
- Join the trend toward tantalizing tee-totaling
- Enjoy happier hours
- Improve your relationships
- Live a joy-filled healthier life.

As fellow New Zealand psychologist and television personality Nigel Latta says, "It's also interesting, don't you think, that given the alcohol industry thinks education is so important, their contribution to 'education' of the public is so... well... limp. They don't even bother to put any real resources into 'education' even though they say it will make a difference."

This was my motivation for writing this book, and for sharing the recipes that have worked for me, my friends and family and my clients in the quest for sobriety.

We have to be the change we want to see. Part of this involves passing on to others the knowledge that I've learned.

My hope is that you step into living sober joyfully. Despite any trepidation, fear or worry, you may feel, my wish is that you'll discover that learning to control alcohol is a pleasure that you never forget to enjoy.

BLAME YOUR BRAIN?

Why do we over-drink? The answer, some neuroscientists believe, lies not in our bellies, but in our brains.

A team of New Zealand scientists has recently begun a new study that aims to pinpoint a 'sensory fingerprint' behind the urge to eat for pleasure. Their findings appear to apply equally to alcohol.

"Eating (and drinking) is a multi-sensory experience, where the taste, smell, appearance and even sound of food are integrated to give pleasure," says Dr. Mei Peng, of Otago University's Department of Food Science.

Some people are particularly susceptible to eating (and drinking) for pleasure, or what's termed hedonic pleasure, says Peng. These differences are thought to be related to brain networks related to rewards, add alcohol to the mix and this makes fighting against our desire to over-indulge a challenging task.

But we can trick our brains and stimulate the reward networks by losing the booze, and plying ourselves with all the other sensory inputs which alcohol barons know make us attracted and addicted to their products. Things like bright, tantalizing colors; sensuously delicious smells; sparkling water bubbling over cool crystal; the warm, sultry feel of a well-rounded glass, cupped in your hand, simultaneously warming your drink.

Plus, alcohol is basically sugar, with more kilojoules. We know how addictive sugar is, but this time we'll get a natural high with plenty of fruits and no booze—and no poisonous ethanol (the ingredient found in beer, wine and spirits that causes drunkness and destroys your brain cells.)

Instead of pickled pretend prettiness you'll reap the benefits of mindful sobriety and beat the drug barons at their own game. Fun!

ABOUT THESE RECIPES

Organized into two volumes, Spring/Summer, and Fall/Winter, this book is a series of carefully curated fun and healthy alcohol alternatives. *Mind Over Mojitos* guides you through a variety of different mock-tail recipes and booze-free alternatives that will make your tastebuds sing and send your dopamine levels soaring.

I've chosen a range of wonderfully refreshing drinks, particularly during the summertime, which are great for picnics or barbeques or just enjoying around the home. Many contain seasonal fruits and berries, are thirst-quenching and also pack some vitamins. Perfect for people who don't like drinking or are not of legal drinking age.

There are two kinds of wintery yet festive drinks to guzzle during the cooler seasons: sparkly and fun mixes that utilize winter fruit, and those that are warm and cozy.

Enjoy this selection, or channel your own mixologist and create your own.

Don't forget, if you ever find yourself in a bar and at a loss for what to drink, or you want to fit in, simply ask for a mocktail (which is what I did when I got the bar staff to create the Virgin Island Fox recipe in this book). Or order a look-alike drink in a fancy glass.

Voila! You'll blend in without having to give everyone a lengthy spiel or justify why you're not drinking alcohol.

Be prepared—plan your booze-free alternative ahead of time and you'll never default to drinking alcohol simply because there was nothing else.

If you create something tasty please share in the dedicated Facebook group where you'll find plenty of thirsty booze-free devotees —https://www.facebook.com/YourBeautifulMindControlAlcoholBoo k

Drinking a non-alcoholic drink should be a fun, sensual and pleasurable experience. Before we dive deeper into some luscious recipes lets clarify what I mean by sobriety, remind yourself of why you need to lose the booze, and then look at the importance of giving good glass. And yes, we will have fun!

WHAT IS SOBRIETY?

Sobriety is more than being teetotal. It's more than fighting a daily battle with your willpower. It's more than the number of drinks you do, or don't knockback.

Sobriety actually means not drinking alcohol in excess, being intoxicated, or drunk.

Dictionary.com defines sobriety as, "the state or quality of being sober; temperance or moderation, especially in the use of alcoholic beverages."

Sobriety does NOT mean abstinence, as some organizations like Alcoholics Anonymous take it to mean.

"'Sobriety' is a word whose 12-step misuse now pervades our entire culture, along with ruining addiction treatment," says addiction expert Dr. Stanton Peele.

"In fact, the DSM psychiatric manual, unbeknownst to virtually everyone who uses it, including even experts who write about it, contains no abstinence criterion for recovery (actually called remission)," Stanton says.

The real issue to focus on is addiction—something, along with dependence, I explore in my book *Your Beautiful Mind: Control Alcohol, Discover Freedom, Find Happiness and Change Your Life*—integrating neuroscience, cognitive therapy, proven tools and teachings to help people suffering from alcohol dependence and addiction win the battle.

Sobriety is about controlling alcohol and living life on your terms.

Mind Over Mojitos and the enticing alcohol-free drink recipes in this book will empower and enable you to more easily make positive choices again and again.

Let's look at why sobriety is sexy and what living sober will do for you.

YOU BOOZE, YOU LOSE

Many people mistakenly believe drinking alcohol will increase their happiness. But alcohol is a depressant and in large quantities is draining on your body and mind.

Experience may have already taught you that too much booze muddles the mind, ignites aggression, reduces responsiveness, and ultimately depresses.

It's also hard to quit—alcohol is one of the most addictive legalized drugs on the planet.

It's also a well-documented neurotoxin—a toxic substance that inhibits, damages, and destroys the cells and tissues of your nervous system.

To bounce back from depression, anxiety and stress many people limit their drinking or consciously decide not to touch a drop. Keeping their resolve often takes extraordinary willpower.

Author and public speaker Deepak Chopra gave up drinking. "I liked it too much," he once said. Steven King, after almost losing his family and destroying his writing career, managed to quit.

Other people like Amy Winehouse devastatingly never made it. At only 27, she died of alcohol poisoning in 2011.

The risk of suicide also increases for stressed people who turn to drink. As I've already discussed, alcohol abuse and excessive drinking is a major cause of anxiety and depression, impairs mental reasoning and critical thinking—increasing the likelihood of making tragic and often impulsive choices.

Risking destroying your career, ruining your relationships, sacrificing your sanity, and in the extreme, taking your life, is a massive price to pay for a mistaken belief that to be happy, or to numb your anxiety, or cope with stress you need to drink more booze.

Bounce beautifully through life by exploring your relationship to drink and approaching it more mindfully.

If you're not in the mood to quit for good consider a period of sobriety. Instead of focusing on what you may be giving up, turn your mind to what you may gain—a better, more energized version of yourself.

Mind Over Mojitos will inspire your quest for success. Let's take a closer look at the growing trend and life-changing magic of mindful drinking.

MINDFUL DRINKING

"No Beers, Who Cares (BWC) isn't about making anyone feel bad about drinking. It's a movement towards shifting attitudes around how and why we drink, and helping people become more aware of their beliefs and habits and having a freaking good time doing so."

~ Claire Robbie, founder No Beers, Who Cares

ROBBIE DESCRIBES HER NO BEERS, Who Cares initiative as not anti-alcohol, but as a pro-mindfulness initiative.

"There's a shift around the world as people understand how incredible life can be without drinking and it's time to bring that high vibration to New Zealand," Robbie (Jack & Olive Retreats, yoga/meditation teacher and journalist) says, "and it's an amazing step towards living more mindfully."

Claire Robbie was a news reporter on TV3's Nightline before a tumultuous time led her to discover the life-changing benefits of yoga and mediation and life without alcohol. At a low point in her life, what started as a hobby became an essential part of her healing process, and as her love for her new practices grew, so did the sense that she had discovered a new vocation.

NBWC isn't about making anyone feel bad about drinking. It's a movement towards shifting attitudes around how and why we drink, and helping people become more aware of their beliefs and habits and having an awesome time doing so. The focus is less about giving something up, but boosting your awareness of how much you gain.

"What we've seen is that giving up alcohol is a keystone habit. A keystone habit is one that unlocks your full well-being potential. Just a few of the benefits of going alcohol-free such as extra energy, motivation, vitality, productivity, money, and time, will begin to pave the way to the life you have always dreamed of," Robbie says.

How can you approach alcohol more mindfully? What might you be giving up by going alcohol free? How much might you gain?

What are you prepared to change in your life? What would stop you? Read on for further incentives on why sobriety is good for you.

WHAT CAN SOBRIETY DO?

Many people struggle to control alcohol because they're not motivated by sobriety. But being sober isn't just about not drinking.

Sobriety is achieved by putting energy and effort toward something you really desire. It's not about saying 'no' to alcohol, and more about saying 'yes!' to living a beautiful life.

There's nothing sexy about drinking too much, slurring your words, staggering around 'legless' or being angrily argumentative. And it's definitely not sexy to puke over yourself, or end up shagging a stranger because you've drunk way too much.

Why do you want to control your drinking?

Knowing why you want something is just as important as knowing what you want.

The many benefits of reducing your alcohol intake, or not drinking at all, include:

✓ A stronger ability to focus on your goals and dreams

✓ Improved confidence and self-esteem

✓ Increased productivity

✓ Increased memory, mental performance, and decision-making

✓ Better control of your emotions

✓ Sweeter relationships

✓ Greater intuition and spiritual intelligence

✓ Authentic happiness

✓ Improved finances

✓ Reduces dehydration and slows down the aging process—making you look and feel sexier for longer!

Not everyone battles with booze. Whether you cut back or eliminate alcohol entirely, the choice is ultimately yours. Only you know the benefits alcohol delivers or the success it destroys. But I'm guessing because you're attracted to this book you're motivated to live happier hours and kick the alcohol habit easily.

Before we take a deep dive into some delicious booze-free recipes, let's take a look at the psychological and sensory benefits of choosing the right glass. If it looks like alcohol, and it's not alcohol you'll be less stressed by peer-pressure to drink and you'll still feel sophisticated.

GIVING GOOD GLASS

Remember it's all in the glass—be sure to pour your drinks into something nice. Drinking a non-alcoholic drink should be a pleasurable experience, and presentation and pleasure go hand-in-hand.

Check out this list below and learn more about the scientific and psychological reasons that it's important to be choosy about your glass.

- The elegance of certain glasses (can give individuals a perception of a finer drinking experience
- The shape of your glass can affect how much and how quickly you drink
- Different glasses bring out the aromas and flavors
- Tall, tapered shapes capture the carbonation and color; glasses with wider bases allows room for swirling to release aromas, which then get trapped at the narrow top. A rounded bottom makes it easy to cup in your hand, simultaneously warming your drink.
- A martini glass's cone shape prevents your ingredients from separating. The long stem also ensures your hands won't

affect the temperature of the drink. As a bonus, the martini glass is sexy no matter who's holding it!

- Champagne coupes, the champagne flutes of our grandparents' generation look elegant, plus the stem keeps your drink cool
- The highball glass is ideal for carbonated mocktails. It's best to keep less surface liquid exposed to air—the more exposed, the quicker the carbonation will evaporate, leaving you with a flat drink.
- Lowball glasses are ideal for high-intensity drinks served on the rocks because they average two to four ounces. Nice since drinking a two-ounce mocktail in a 10-ounce highball may feel a little weak.
- Tulip or white wine glass. Small, slender, tulip-shaped glassware, help slow down any rise in temperature from the chilled beverages, while the stem of the glass allows you to hold your drink without your hands heating it up—keeping your drink cooler for longer.
- Warmer drinks should be served in larger, bowl-shaped glasses to increase surface area and allow for more aroma release.
- Tulip champagne flutes. The narrow, tulip-shaped flute is a familiar drinking vessel at weddings and toast-worthy occasions for holding your celebratory bubbly. The carbonation is the major reason behind the shape. The glass helps retain Champagne's trademark carbonation, and the bowl is also designed to visually highlight the rising bubbles. Perfect for non-alcoholic champagne mixes and carbonated drinks with fizz.
- Stemless glass. With their clean design and easy-to-clean shape (no worries about shattering a delicate stem here!), stemless glasses are best for drinks served at room temp since your hands holding the glass can unintentionally heat up cooler drinks.

Size matters! Small can be beautiful. A tiny crystal long stemmed-glass is one of my favorite glasses to enjoy a wee sip of beer or wine on special occasions. Remember sobriety is not about abstinence but about being in control of your drinking.

But, with so many tasty alternatives to booze, you'll soon find, as I did, that you'll kick the drink habit easily.

Are you ready to discover easy recipes for happier hours of joy- filled sober living? Part One starts with spring and summer, alcohol- free alternatives to enjoy. Recipes for the cooler months follows in Part Two.

First up, my personal favorite—Virgin Island Fox!

PART I

NON-ALCOHOLIC DRINKS FOR SPRING & SUMMER

1

VIRGIN ISLAND FOX

A mocktail version of a classic created for me by the hip-cool folk at Charlotte's Kitchen in Pahia, The Bay of Islands, New Zealand—my spiritual home. An elegant and restrained cocktail with subtle richness balanced with lovely zest.

Ingredients

- 1 tsp orange marmalade
- 90mls grapefruit juice
- 30mls lime juice
- 15 mls sugar syrup
- Ice

Method

- Add all ingredients except the ice into a mixer

- Single strain over ice into a wine glass
- Garnish – grapefruit

2

PASSION FRUIT BUBBLY

Guilt-free sparkle when passion fruit is in season and mixed with sparkling wine for a festive drink.

Ingredients

- 1/2 Lemon, juice of
- 1 small bunch of mint
- 2 cups caster sugar
- 1/2 tsp Salt
- 1 cup of ice
- 1 bottle sparkling wine or soda water
- 2 cups water
- 1 tsp citric acid
- 1 cup of passion fruit pulp (fresh or tinned)

Method

- Place all the ingredients in a saucepan and stir over a medium heat until the sugar is dissolved

- Bring to the boil, take of the heat and allow to cool
- Taste to see if the cordial needs some extra lemon juice
- Serve I part cordial to 3 parts bubbly over lots of ice and garnish with fresh mint
- Keep any leftover cordial in a clean and airtight container, refrigerated for up to 4 weeks
- Makes about 750ml of cordial

3

PASSION FRUIT POWER PUNCH

Perfect for a hot day and easy to mix. Displays aromas of bright fruit and hints of citrus. Rich texture and a sparkling twist. Finishes just like an Indian Summer—long and lovely.

Ingredients

- 1 cup of passion fruit pulp (fresh or tinned)
- I good handful of mint leaves (plus extras to serve)
- I squeezed lime (1 lime per 4 drinks)
- I cup of sparkling water per drink

Method

Combine passion fruit, lime juice and mint over ice and then top with sparkling water. Serve with extra mint in the glass.

4

MOSMO

This citrus-infused remake of the classic Cosmopolitan (made famous by Sex and the City) was invented especially for me by the Parisian bartender at Charlotte's Kitchen in the beautiful Bay of Islands.

Ingredients

- 90mls orange juice
- 90mls apple juice
- 30mls cranberry juice
- dash of lime
- Ice

Method

- Add all ingredients except the ice into a mixer

- Double strain over ice into a large, chilled cocktail glass
- Garnish – orange zest

5

H2O CLEAN & COLLECTED

When you think premixed drinks, do you think "loaded with alcohol, neurotoxins, carcinogens, sugar, additives and a whole lot of unnecessary calories?" Well so did we.

This thought-enhancing drink is guaranteed to satisfy the thirst of those who want a lot of indulgence, while still embracing a healthy lifestyle—H2O Clean & Collected is created for people like you and me, who care about what we put in our bodies and are sick of artificial highs, and alcoholic sugar-loaded drinks bloating our shelves and stomachs.

Full of personality, it is light bodied, with incisive lemon/lime flavors, a seductive balance of acidity, guilt-free sweetness (zero sugar, zero carbs, zero preservatives) with a lasting finish.

Ingredients

- Water (fresh rain or spring water if available)
- Ice
- Slice of organic lemon or lime

Method

Pour water into your favorite stunning glass, I prefer crystal and sometimes a lovely champagne flute is elegant.

Garnish with fruit or add a wee drop of freshly squeezed juice or your fav healthy syrup.

If bubbles make your soul sing, whip out your SodaStream, or (RTD) bottled soda, pump up the volume and enjoy a natural high.

100% clean and natural!

Thank you to Russ Perry, author of *The Sober Entrepreneur* for sharing his go-to-drink of choice—sparkling water, with a dash of lime. Sometimes the simpler things in life are the best.

In fact, this is so good perhaps we should bottle it!

6

BLUEBERRY AND MAPLE MOJITO

Stunning and stimulating! Exotic in style, clean and crisp, zesty on the palate with aromas of mint and limes. A complete winner and sure to impress even the most discerning drinker.

Ingredients

- 8-10 mint leaves, plus more for garnish
- 1 tsp fresh lime juice
- 1 tbsp. good-quality maple syrup
- 1/3 cup organic blueberry juice-no added sugar
- 1/2 cup soda
- Frozen blueberries, for garnish

Method

. . .

Add the mint leaves to a glass (size depends on how much you want). Muddle well until the mint releases its flavor.

Add the lime juice, maple syrup, blueberry juice and soda to the glass and stir until all the ingredients are well-combined.

Serves 1, prep time 5 minutes

7

TAMARILLO THYME SPRITZER

This zesty drink created by my partner, Lorenzo, ticks all the right boxes—quirky, original and something completely different. A delicious drink that sits perfectly in the long lazy days of our new world New Zealand summer. More than flavor it smells good too.

Ingredients

- 3 organic tamarillo (tree tomato)
- Soda water
- I tsp brown sugar
- Sprigs of thyme

Method

Combine crushed tamarillo and thyme with brown sugar over ice and then top with sparkling water. Serve with extra thyme in the glass.

8

VIRGIN STRAWBERRY DAIQUIRI

When it's summertime the strawberries are easy! Here are a few yummy recipes for virgin strawberry daiquiris. The berries are thirst-quenching and also pack vivacious vitamins. The palate is mouth-watering and intense from the very first sip right through to the finish.

Ingredients

- 1 ounce of fresh lime juice
- 3 ounces of fresh strawberries
- 2 teaspoons of sugar (or more if the strawberries are tart)
- Cracked ice

Method

- Fill your blender with the cracked ice. Add the lime juice, strawberries and sugar and blend until completely smooth.

- If the mixture is too thick, add a little water.
- When you're finished, pour the drink into a chilled glass and garnish it with a fresh strawberry.

Virgin Daiquiri with Soda

Ingredients

- 2 large strawberries without the tops
- 1/4 cup sugar
- 1 tablespoon of lime juice
- 3/4 cup of lemon-lime soda, such as 7-UP or Sprite
- 4 medium ice cubes

Instructions

- In a blender, blend the strawberries, sugar, lime juice, and lemon-lime soda.
- Add the ice cubes and blend all the ingredients until they are smooth. If the drink is too thick, add more soda.

9

GRAPEFRUIT HONEY GINGER SODA

Light and tangy fizz, sweetened with honey, not sugar, and a hint of ginger provides a note of warmth in cooler months.

This recipe is for a syrup that you can mix with carbonated water (store-bought or homemade). It has a bittersweet, grown-up flavor from the use of grapefruit zest and a slight spiciness from the addition of fresh ginger.

Ingredients

- Zest of 1 large pink or red grapefruit (preferably organic)
- 1 cup freshly-squeezed pink or red grapefruit juice (from about 1 large grapefruit; if necessary, top off with water to make 1 cup
- 3/4 cup mild-flavored honey
- 1/4 cup chopped fresh ginger
- Carbonated water, for serving

Method

Combine the grapefruit zest, grapefruit juice, honey, and ginger in a small saucepan over medium heat. Boil for 2 minutes, stirring to dissolve the honey.

Remove from heat and let cool. Strain the syrup through a sieve into a clean container and discard the solids.

To serve, spoon 2 tablespoons of syrup into an 8-ounce glass, top with carbonated water, and stir to combine. Taste and add more syrup, if desired.

The syrup can be refrigerated for up to 1 week.

Looking beyond soda, the syrup can also be used in cocktails or drizzled over fresh fruit salad.

Source:

https://www.thekitchn.com/recipe-grapefruit-ginger-honey-soda-syrup-recipes-from-the-kitchn-198705

10

THE MEG RYAN: A BRIGHT & BUBBLY BLENDED BERRY DRINK

You will love this drink—just like one of the world's most adored actresses. A fun, frivolous, fantastic winner. Pure delight.

Ingredients

- 1 cup berries (whatever is in season)
- 1 tsp lemon juice
- 2 tbsp honey
- 1 cup soda water

Method

Add berries, lemon juice, and honey to a blender and combine until smooth. Add soda water and pulse until combined. If using frozen berries, you may add ingredients all at once, but you might need to add a dash of soda water at the end to bubble things back up to our tongue tingling standards.

That's all there is to it, nothing fancy, nothing shaken, nothing stirred and nothing strained (unless you really, really want to). Make sure to pulse some water through your blender when done so clean up is extra easy and you don't even have to worry about dishes. All you'll have left to do is frolic around looking fabulous and smiling making people everywhere love you. Seriously, the drink has powers!

Source:

https://www.thekitchn.com/recipe-a-bright-bubbly-blended-124969

11

PINEAPPLE CHAMOMILE TEA

Refreshing, calming and restorative—what's not to love about this nifty, nerve-enhancing mix. A luminous golden glow in a glass, layered with chamomile and honey to finish. Enjoy!

Ingredients

- 4 Chamomile tea bags
- 1 1/2 cups of water
- 1/2 cup frozen pineapple chunks
- 2 1/2 cups crushed ice
- 2 tablespoon chopped basil
- Honey, to taste

Method

Boil the water in a small saucepan. Remove the pan from the heat, add the tea bags and steep them for 2-3 minutes. Allow the tea to cool.

Add the cooled tea, 1 cup of the ice, the pineapple, and the honey to a blender and blend together. Stir in the basil leaves. (It will be frothy so let it sit for a couple minutes so the contents of the blender can settle. The longer you let the flavors come together the better the tea will taste.

Evenly fill two glasses with the rest of the crushed ice, and pour the tea over. Serve!

Source:

http://chocolateforbasil.com/pineapple-chamomile-tea/

12

VIRGIN MOJITO

Easy to mix and a refreshing to drink on a simmering hot day. Fresh, bright and crisp. Feel the love in this powerful, tight and elegant perennial favorite. Wow!

Ingredients

- 1/3 cup Apple juice
- 1/3 cup Sparkling water
- 1 whole lime, sliced and quartered
- 3 mint leaves
- 1 teaspoon sugar

Method

- Muddle the lime, sugar and mint leaves until they are just releasing the juice

- Place ice in a glass, add muddled mixture and pour in apple juice
- Top with sparkling water and stir
- Garnish with a slice of lime and mint leaf and serve

Source:

https://www.soberjulie.com/2016/06/mojito-recipe/

13

RASPBERRY MINT JULEP

Raspberries, mint, simple syrup and ginger ale combine to make what may be the BEST ever non-alcoholic Mint Julep! Full bodied with a rich texture and a long, soft, finish. Yummy, can we all have another serving, please!

Ingredients

- 2 teaspoons simple syrup (equal parts water and sugar, cook on high heat until it boils and cool before using)
- 6 large raspberries
- 3 mint leaves
- 2 ounces Ginger Ale
- Crushed Ice
- Mint leaf for garnish

Method

- Begin by adding the simple syrup and raspberries to glass and muddle gently (muddle=press down with flat end of spoon or muddler)
- Next, add mint leaves and muddle to bruise them slightly
- Add 2 ounces of Ginger Ale to glass
- Fill with crushed ice and add a straw and mint leaf for garnish.

SOURCE:

https://www.soberjulie.com/2016/07/raspberry-mint-julep-recipe-non-alcoholic/

14

BASIL MOJITO ICED TEA

Amazing Mojito Iced Tea! Black Tea and basil fuse together to create this delicious and refreshing iced tea. Perfect for dinner parties! While this recipe was created by the good folk at Lipton there's nothing stopping you from recreating it with your own fave tea.

Ingredients

- 4 cups water
- 2 Lipton® Iced Tea Brew Family Size Tea Bags
- 4 sprigs fresh basil leaves
- 1/4 cup lime juice
- 2 cups chilled seltzer

Method

- Pour boiling water over Lipton® Iced Tea Brew Family Size

Tea Bags. Brew 5 minutes. Remove Tea Bags and squeeze; cool 20 minutes.

- Put basil into a 2-quart pitcher and gently crush with wooden spoon. Stir in brewed Tea and lime juice. Chill until ready to serve. Just before serving, stir in seltzer. Pour into ice-filled glasses and sweeten as desired.

Source:

https://www.lipton.com/us/en/tea-recipes/basil-mojito-iced-tea.html

15

VIRGIN SCREWDRIVER

Looks like the real deal and only you need to know that it's both alcohol and guilt free—not to mention so much lower in calories.

Ingredients

- Orange juice (freshly squeezed if available)
- Soda Water
- Ice

Method

- Add ice to preferred glass, suggest high ball or long
- Pour orange juice over ice
- Top with soda water
- Decorate with a slice or twist of orange and or a cherry

Serves 1, prep time less than 5 minutes

NOTE: use orange juice & soda in a ratio that suits your taste, the soda simply makes the orange juice look like it is has been mixed with vodka giving it that diluted look

Source: Niki Firth emailed me this recipe after reading the first edition of this book.

"As the daughter of an alcoholic father, I am well aware of my own predisposition. When he fought for control, he would drink orange juice on ice, in a highball glass with a splash of soda and a wedge of orange. It looked just like a Screwdriver and no-one ever questioned it."

Moscow Mule, Niki's favorite alcohol-free recipe, follows.

16

VIRGIN MOSCOW MULE

A refreshing taste of lime with the added zest of ginger but no hangover. World class!

Ingredients

- 1 Lime (quartered)
- Ginger beer (not dry or ale)
- Ice, lightly smashed
- Ginger toffee (optional—recipe follows)

Method

- Add ice and 2 lime quarters to a mug style glass
- Muddle lime and ice to release juice and flavor
- Top glass with ginger beer and serve with 2 straws
- Decorate with clapped mint leaves and a slice of lime or alternatively ...

- Decorate with some smashed ginger toffee (optional)

Serves 2, prep time less than 10 minutes

Ginger Toffee

Ingredients

- 1 cup caster sugar
- 1/4 cup water
- Fresh ginger, peeled and finely but roughly diced, use enough to suit your taste

Instructions

- Stir sugar and water in a saucepan over a low heat until the sugar has dissolved; do NOT try to boil the mixture until all the sugar is completely dissolved
- Add ginger and increase heat to bring mixture to the boil; use a wet pastry brush to wipe down any sugar crystals that form up the side of the pan
- Bring mixture to the boil and continue boiling until mixture turns golden; do not let it burn
- Remove from heat; mixture will continue to bubble and color will enrich
- Allow mixture to cool slightly but not set; pour a thin layer onto a baking sheet covered with baking paper
- Once completely hard, lightly smash toffee, into large shards which will suit the chosen glass size to decorate Virgin Moscow Mule
- Store remaining shards in an airtight container; lasts ages.

Source: Niki Firth

17

PRE-MIXES & RTD'S

Whether you're heading to the beach, off to a BBQ, heading for a night out, or looking for a fridge staple, there's a wide array of easy-easy pre-mixed no-booze mixes to enjoy. Here are just a few of my many fave pre-bottled sophisticated drinks. Unleash your creativity and mix your own.

Pre-Mixed

- **Mac's Sparkling Sodas.** Available in Feijoa, Pear & Elderflower; Lemonade & Rhubarb; Ginger Beer; and Mandarin, Lime & Bitters; these non-alcoholic delights are a passion-fuelled ingeniously Kiwi mix of flavors that will tantalize the taste buds of even the most discerning drinker. With 40% less sugar than normal soft drinks, Mac's Sparkling Sodas are perfect for the conscientious soda drinker. Mac's Sparkling Sodas are very grown up.
- **Fever-Tree Aromatic Tonic Water.** Aromatic botanicals, including cardamom, pimento berry and ginger, blend with

the gentle bitterness of South American angostura bark to create a delicious, unique tonic water. This pink aromatic tonic can be enjoyed a sophisticated drink on its own.

- **Grapetiser.** Bursting with a distinct grape scent and flavor, this lightly sparkling red or white grape juice contains no added sugar, preservatives or artificial colorants. Deliciously good and perfect on its own!
- **Lipton Iced-tea.** Join the cult of chilling tea with these recipes: https://www.lipton.com/us/en/tea-recipes.html
- **San Pellegrino.** The finest Italian sparkling natural mineral water preferred by top chefs and fine dining lovers all around the world. Sparkling or flavored? Learn more here: https://www.sanpellegrino.com/intl/en/
- **Aroha (New Zealand) Cordials, Sparking and Stills.** Refreshing elderflower infused drinks with fabulous flavors, including Rhubarb, Gooseberry, Ginger Honey & Lemon, Wild Rosehip, Quince & Lime, Elderflower & Greencurrant. Discover more here: http://www.arohadrinks.co.nz/aroha-drinks
- Other no-alcohol alternatives, including grown-up cordials, ginger beers and pre-mixes can easily be found near the children's aisle in any supermarket

Mix Your Own

In addition to the recipes you've discovered throughout this book, below are just a few easy-peasy drinks you can whip up with minimal fuss:

- Sparkling water on the rocks with a twist of lime
- Ginger Beer, with a teaspoon of marmalade, on the rocks
- Sparkling water with a dash of fresh fruit or syrup

Remember it's all in the glass—be sure to pour your drinks into something nice.

18

APPLE 'NO-JITO'

A mocktail version of the classic Mojito created for me March 2018 by the hip-cool ladies (Meghan, Analiese and the waitress, Georgia) at Charlotte's Kitchen in Pahia, The Bay of Islands, New Zealand. A refreshing, zesty cocktail with subtle sweetness balanced with a little tickle.

Ingredients

- 45mls apple juice
- 15mls lemon juice
- 15mls lime juice
- 30 mls sugar syrup
- Soda to fill your chosen glass
- Mint
- Ice

Method

- Add all ingredients except the ice into a mixer
- Double strain over ice into a large, 1/2 pint glass (that's fun!)
- Garnish – mint

PART II

NON-ALCOHOLIC DRINKS FOR WINTER & FALL

There are two kinds of wintery yet festive drinks to guzzle during the cooler seasons: sparkly and fun mixes that utilize winter fruit, and those that are hot and cozy.

19

KIWI FRUIT KISS

The choice of available fresh fruit to put in a glass dwindles in winter and this recipe provides a welcome change. The kiwi's distinctive markings make it look like an exotic emerald green and black butterfly. Add the bright and fresh hints of crisp apple and zesty lime, and this drink guarantees to make your spirit fly. Beautiful!

Ingredients

- 2 ripe Kiwis
- 150 ml apple juice
- Optional: squeeze of lime

Method

Peel the kiwi fruit, chop into large chunks and puree in a blender. Stir in the apple juice and lime and serve.

20

MULLED CRANBERRY APPLE CIDER

Enjoy this delicious family-friendly cider recipe for a healthy alcohol- and sugar-free drink that everyone can enjoy. Cosy, warm and spiced, this plain apple cider is dressed up with cranberries, which give this seasonal drink a lovely, rosy tartness.

Ingredients

- 2 cups unsweetened cranberry juice blend or cranberry cocktail
- 6 cups unsweetened apple cider or apple juice
- Peel of 1 orange, cut into large strips
- 1-inch piece of ginger, peeled and sliced
- 2 (3-inch) cinnamon sticks
- 4 whole allspice berries
- 4 whole cloves
- Optional sweeteners: honey, brown sugar, or sucanat
- Optional garnishes: cinnamon sticks, orange slices, fresh cranberries

Method

Place all ingredients in a large pot and bring to a boil. Reduce heat and simmer, partially covered, for 30 minutes. Strain and serve warm.

Whether you sweeten it will depend on personal preference and the juices you use.

Serve in individual cups or a crockpot with festive garnishes like cinnamon sticks, fresh cranberries, and orange slices.

Source:

https://www.thekitchn.com/recipe-mulled-cranberry-apple-cider-recipes-from-the-kitchn-180627

21

CRANBERRY FIZZ PUNCH

Strong, tangy syrup of fresh cranberries, ginger, and rosemary, infused in cranberry juice. An absolutely splendid drop which is sure to be a crowd pleaser.

This recipe takes time to build several layers but you'll be rewarded with stronger and richer flavors like those found in a great cocktail.

Ingredients

For the Cranberry-Rosemary Syrup:

- 2 1/2 cups fresh or frozen cranberries (12-ounce bag)
- 2 ounces fresh ginger, skin on and sliced (about 1/2 cup)
- 1/2 cup sugar
- 3 cups cranberry juice cocktail, no sugar added
- 2 large sprigs fresh rosemary
- 4 to 7 cups tonic water

For the Cranberry Punch Mix:

- 1/4 ounce black tea leaves (decaffeinated if desired)
- 4 cups boiling water
- 3 cups Cranberry Rosemary Syrup
- 1/4 cup pomegranate molasses, without any added sweeteners
- 1/4 cup non-alcoholic orange bitters, such as Fee Brothers

Method

To make the Cranberry-Rosemary Syrup:

Blitz the cranberries and ginger in a food processor until roughly chopped, then mix with the sugar and cranberry juice cocktail in a 3-quart saucepan. Bring to a boil, then add the rosemary. Lower the heat and simmer for 5 minutes. Let cool, ideally overnight in the refrigerator. Strain through a fine mesh strainer and discard the solids. You should have about 3 cups of thin syrup. Syrup can be refrigerated for up to 1 week or frozen.

To prepare **the Cranberry Punch Mix:**

Place the tea leaves in a large heatproof bowl. Pour the boiling water over them and steep for 3 minutes. Strain out the leaves, and whisk in the Cranberry Rosemary Syrup, pomegranate molasses, and orange bitters.

Refrigerate the punch mix for at least 4 hours, or overnight.

Non-Alcoholic Cranberry Fizz

To serve a non-alcoholic drink, stir the punch mix together with 6 to 7 cups tonic water. Serve over ice. Makes about 18 x 6-ounce servings.

. . .

SOURCE: https://www.thekitchn.com/cocktail-or-mocktail-recipe-festive-cranberry-fizz-recipes-from-the-kitchn-198415

22

SPICED APPLE CIDER

Spice up fresh, local apple cider with warm cinnamon and cloves. Fine acid structure, rich color and warm tones.

Ingredients

- 1 gallon fresh apple cider
- 10 cinnamon sticks
- 5 star anise pods
- 3 teaspoons whole cloves
- Orange slices for garnish

Method

Pour the cider into a large pot and simmer with the spices for 10 to 15 minutes. If you want, tie the spices up in cheesecloth for easy removal later—or just let people deal with cloves in their drinks. Garnish with a slice of orange.

Source:

https://www.thekitchn.com/recipe-spiced-apple-cider-32035

23

HOT MULLED APPLE CIDER & ORANGE SANGRIA

Simmer apple cider and orange juice together with traditional mulling spices, fresh fruit, honey, and slices of spicy fresh ginger for a sangria-like twist on regular mulled apple cider. A luscious and full finish.

Ingredients

- 4 (1/4-inch-thick) slices fresh ginger, smashed
- 12 whole cloves
- 6 whole allspice berries
- 1/2 gallon (8 cups) apple cider or unfiltered apple juice
- 2 cups freshly squeezed orange juice
- 1/3 cup honey
- 1 medium navel orange, cut into 1/4-inch-thick rounds
- 1 medium tart apple, cut crosswise into 1/4-inch-thick slices
- 1 medium lemon, cut into 1/4-inch-thick rounds
- 4 (3-inch) cinnamon sticks
- *For serving:* Cinnamon sticks

Method

Place the ginger, cloves, and allspice in a double layer of cheesecloth and tie together with kitchen string to form a pouch. Place in a 4-quart or larger slow cooker, add the remaining ingredients, and stir to combine. Cover and heat on the LOW setting until simmering and the flavors meld, about 3 hours. Keep on the warm setting for up to 3 hours.

Serve as is, or place 1 cup wassail in a mug and add 1 to 1 1/2 ounces liquor if desired. Garnish with cinnamon sticks if desired.

Recipe Notes

Storage: Strain out the fruit and spices and store leftovers in an airtight container in the refrigerator for up to 5 days. Reheat over low heat.

Source:

https://www.thekitchn.com/recipe-wassail-punch-133422

24

ASIAN PEAR SPARKLER

This Asian pear sparkler is smooth and refreshing with an enticing undercurrent of warm autumn flavors and mellow warmth. Rosemary and ginger with discrete tastes of honey finish this splendid drop.

Ingredients

- 1 cup freshly pressed Asian pear juice*
- 1 teaspoon lemon juice
- 3/4 cup honey
- 1/4 cup sugar
- 1 (4-inch) sprig fresh rosemary
- 1 (1-inch) piece fresh ginger, peeled and cut into coins
- Small grating of fresh nutmeg
- Ice
- Soda water

Method

Combine pear juice, lemon juice, honey, sugar, rosemary, ginger, and nutmeg in a saucepan over medium heat. Bring to a boil, then simmer on low heat for 5 minutes, stirring to dissolve the sugars.

Remove from heat and let stand 30 minutes. Strain the syrup through a fine-mesh strainer and discard the solids. Let syrup cool completely.

To serve, fill an 8-ounce glass halfway with ice cubes, add 3 tablespoons of syrup, fill with soda water, and stir. Add more syrup for a sweeter or stronger flavor.

*Note: Use the most flavorful Asian pear you can find; Hosui is a consistently sweet variety. Making 1 cup of juice requires about 1 (12-ounce) pear, peeled and cored. If using a juicer, follow manufacturer's instructions to extract the juice and discard the pulp. If using blender or food processor, puree the pear until smooth, strain through a fine-mesh strainer, and discard the solids. If you wind up with a little less than 1 cup, top it up with water.

Source: https://www.thekitchn.com/drink-recipe-as-161626

A FEW LAST WORDS

I hope this book has provided encouragement and empowered your tenacity to control alcohol and enjoy a spell of mindful sobriety.

If you continue to exercise self-care and embrace mindful drinking then this unpredictable and fascinating life will manifest in favorable outcomes—for you, for those you love, and those drawn to you because of the beauty, power, and magic of the life you have created.

Let the beauty you love be the life that you live. Take care of your- self and your heart, and nourish your mind, body, and soul.

You've discovered a melody of sexy, wonderfully refreshing and healthy alcohol-free alternatives to booze. The world is awash with stimulating, life enhancing alternatives. Continue to enjoy this carefully curated selection, or channel your own mixologist and invent your own.

And don't forget—if you discover or create any tasty alcohol-free recipes please share in the dedicated Facebook group where you'll find plenty of thirsty booze-free devotees —https://www.facebook.com/Sobrietyexperiment/

If you haven't downloaded your free Find Your Passion workbook, get instant access here—https://worklifesolutions.lpages.co/free-find-your-passion-workbook-control-alcohol

To your health and happiness, and with love,

P.S. I truly hope you enjoyed *Mind Over Mojitos*. I'm excited about the possibilities to take this simple but profound message of self-empowered choice and sobriety into the world.

This book in the Mindful Sobriety series, is a companion guide to *Your Beautiful Mind: Control Alcohol, Discover Freedom, Find Happiness and Change Your Life*—integrating neuroscience, cognitive therapy, proven tools, and teachings to help people overcome alcohol dependence and addiction. *Your Beautiful Mind: Control Alcohol* offers a five-phase plan using success principles, goal setting, visualizations, neuroscience, and cognitive therapies to assist readers in identifying the reasons for drinking, defeating the dread of quitting, cultivating gratitude, strengthening your spiritual connection, and taking pleasure in self-esteem and confidence-building activities...

Sign up for my newsletter to be the first to know when this and other new books are released, and receive practical tips to live your best life—http://eepurl.com/di-pEf

Be the first to know when my guided meditations and self-hypnosis audios are released, and stay tuned for news of my online courses, webinars and international retreats in exotic, empowering locations.

Sign up here http://eepurl.com/di-pEf

PLEASE LEAVE A REVIEW

Your feedback encourages and sustains me and I love hearing from you.

Show your support. Share how this book has helped you by leaving a REVIEW—Even a one-liner would be helpful.

I recently received an email from a reader who said, "*Your books are a fantastic resource and until now I never even thought to write a review. Going forward I will be reviewing more books. So many great ones out there and I want to support the amazing people that write them.*"

Great reviews also help people find good books.

THANK YOU

PS: If you enjoyed this book, do me a small favour to help spread the word about it and share news of this book with your tribe on Facebook, Twitter and other social networks.

EXCERPT: YOUR BEAUTIFUL MIND: CONTROL ALCOHOL

"A vitally important discussion...
finally a sensible, holistic approach to drinking"

#1 International Bestseller

Your
Beautiful
Mind

Control Alcohol
& Love Life More

By the Author of STRESS LESS

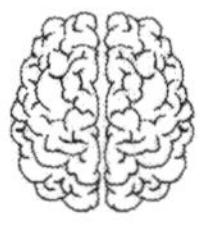

Discover Freedom,
Find Happiness
& Change Your Life

Cassandra Gaisford

PRAISE FOR YOUR BEAUTIFUL MIND

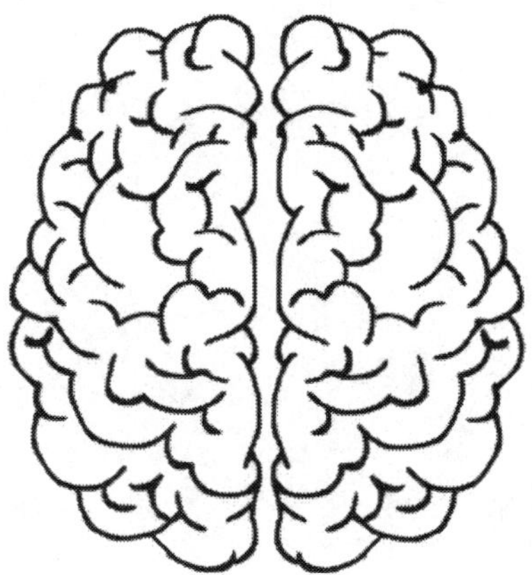

"I work with people and their whanau/families on a daily basis who have, have had or have recovered from Alcohol and Other Drug issues. The damage caused by AOD over use and abuse is enormous and has ongoing negative effects on our society and future generations mainly due to observation and learned behaviours.

I really like the approach that this book takes in not attempting to stop drinking totally. It instead explains and coaches how to manage and cope with consuming alcohol so that the damaging effects may be minimised. This is a very useful supportive book for 'drinkers' and their families.

It is a book that is very easy to read and understand. I really like the quotes, sayings and tools contained therein. This book is much bigger than just the social and familial issues with alcohol – It is in a very big way about 'Your Beautiful Mind'.

It fits very well with my style of practice and that is to start with the basics and move onwards and upwards from there. I see in the book an AHA (awakening, honesty, action) moment in the book. I really get the reference to wisdom (The smart person knows what to say, the wise person knows when to say it) and the associated learning.

I will be recommending this 'must read' book to my clients and their whanau/families and anybody else who will listen."

~ Philipe Eyton, Counsellor, Life and Leadership Coach, BSocP, NZAC

"I like the content of the book a lot. As an ex-drunk who quit for both mental and physical health reasons, it's very affirming. I like her comment that she's yet to meet an ex-drinker who preferred life as a drinker.

I think it will appeal to both people who are considering change and people who have made a change to their drinking and want both affirmation and some information so they can explain why to their friends.

I like its meandering style (it makes me think of sharing in a group). It's too good a message to ignore."

~ Andrew Nicholls

““What an incredibly informative read. I really love how Cassandra has different viewpoints that allow the reader to come to their own conclusions.

Your Beautiful Mind: Control Alcohol and Love Life More is a non-biased informative read based on various facts, research and readings and I feel it is a book that I could pick up time and time again, and that whatever is relevant to me at that time or moment in my life is what I'll be able to take away when I pick it up.

I loved that information was backed up by science and offered rhetorical questions and facts to get the reader thinking, rather than preaching or telling the reader how to do something.

I loved the perception that it is more helpful to heal the root of our cause to drink, rather than try to blindly control alcohol consumption, and that each reader will feel empowered to choose their own method for sobriety rather than feeling like they have to stick to rules. (Who likes rules anyway!?).

Very empowering, honest and thought-provoking.”

~ Libby Wallace, Founder *Soberly*

"One thing that I like about this book is that the author doesn’t trash other recovery programs whether she agrees with them or not. This approach is very different (and refreshing) from other books I’ve read that claim to be the “real or only solution” which involves tearing down other methods in the process, but as Cassandra's book alludes —one form of recovery may work for some people and not others—it depends on the person, their physiology, background, life experience, etc.

“At first, I thought the segments about advertising would be boring but they actually really appealed to the part of me that loves science, facts, and proof. Reading the explanations led to many “Aha!” moments! I also felt so relieved to read there is a sober/not drinking movement going on. I felt relieved and hopeful. How I wish this was going on when I started my own drinking career in my early teens. I'm feeling so grateful to Cassandra for writing it. There is so much vital information packed into this book and I wish fervently that it ends up on the best seller list!"

~ Lisa Ruggiero, Amazon 5-Star Review

"I realised my minimal drinking habit of the past 11 months entered my life gently without any major decision and has brought to my life a feeling of relaxedness, a feeling of self-love, I didn't realise that by the act of less alcohol I have achieved the list of benefits cited in *Your Beautiful Mind*. This chapter allowed me to reflect on my choice and to realise that it was, and is, an act of self-love and that feels very special to me.

"This is a book for anyone who is struggling with alcohol (or even overeating/comfort eating - it can be used for several addictions) as a way to encourage the reader to look at their drinking (or other affliction) in a loving way, encouraging the reader to work with their intelligent self, on a loving level, it offers support, (you don't feel alone), it offers stories of awareness, idea's for moving beyond the clutches of alcohol and experiencing the joy of living a full, creative, and/or self-loving life."

~ Catherine Sloan, Counselor

"I see people that I would love to give this book recommendation to. They need this in their lives-a few of who would not consider, they have any problem with alcohol, nor have any desire to stop drinking - but I liked this book because the message is that you take control of how you steer the ship. You can choose to decrease and manage your drinking or you can choose to omit alcohol altogether from your life.

"Alcohol is abused and I know a few young people (18-25yrs) that haven't a clue of what they're drinking or the impacts on them physically, mentally or emotionally. This is huge. Yet each and every week they are returning to the bottle to find some solace in drinking or in fact getting pissed.

"I love the connection Cassandra shares with herself in this book. The Sobriety Journal she mentions and has created is a fantastic tool - and I would recommend people use conjunction with this book and your own journey- it will do wonders. It's a great reflective tool also to go back to down the track, as Cassandra has openly displayed herself.

"I am quite surprised myself about the new knowledge I gained from what I read in this book. And wondered why when I was drinking did I never stop to consider what I was drinking, what my drink was made of and how- never ever! I can remember thinking, I wonder how many calories are in this beer. Or how much sugar. But never looked it up as such, as I didn't actually want to know at the time. I was in somewhat of a denial. I just wanted to consume it anyway. I quite often was sick on the evening or the next day after a binge.

"So this information needs to be shared and is available in this book. I think that's fantastic. It's not too complex. At first, I wondered if I would see my younger relatives reading this and relating to it. And thought, maybe not. But then when momentum picked up and the diverse realities were seen and heard - I thought it would relate to many soft spots they have and I hopefully allow them to take control of themselves and their drinking.

"Loving what I read. I am seeing some home truths and common vulnerabilities which makes this book relatable to many."

~ Jo-Maitera

"I cold-turkey stopped imbibing alcohol and I've gained twenty years in energy. We all know we don't drink a lot but what an insidious thing nightly alcohol is."

~ Melinda Hammond, Author

DEDICATION

This book is dedicated to three beautiful women:
My grandmother Molly Fairweather
Amy Winehouse
and Venus, the goddess of love

. . .and to three beautiful men:
My father, Graeham Gaisford, from whom I have inherited a deep reverence for holistic medicine
Lorenzo, my life partner who inspired this book and nurtures me daily
and my grandfather, Reg, who taught me to laugh, laugh, laugh—and not take life, or myself, too seriously

Your Beautiful Mind is also dedicated to all the beautiful souls whose lives have been impacted by alcohol...
and to those who became sober warriors, fought their way back from addiction, and inspired us all

THE TRUTHS

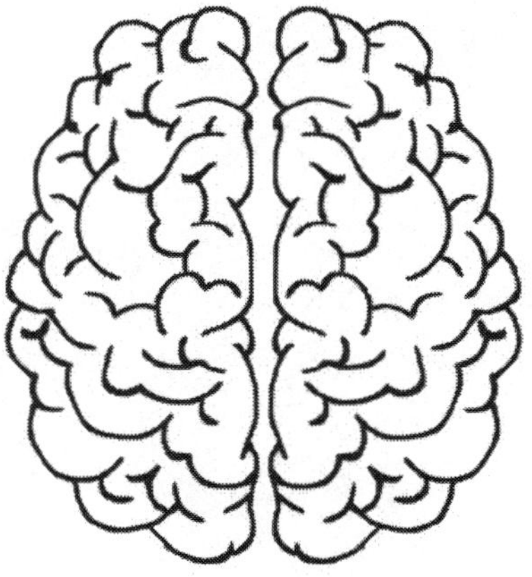

"Science has sometimes been at odds with the notion that laypeople can cure themselves."

~ Jarret Liotta

"Then you shall know the truth, and the truth will set you free."

~ John 8:32

"I have yet to meet a person whose sobriety has made their life worse. I have yet to—but I am open to it. If you find some one please get in touch with me because I would love to have a chat with them and ask them a couple of questions. I have yet to meet a person whose sobriety didn't make a better father, a better friend..."

~ Colin Farrell

"Extremes are to be avoided."

~ Leonardo da Vinci

"When you are full of food and drink an ugly statue sits where your spirit should be."

~ Rumi

"I gave up alcohol in 1980. I enjoyed it far too much, to the point where I frequently get intoxicated. Everything in my life changed for the better when I stopped. It was the right decision."

~ Deepak Chopra

"When I cut out alcohol, my life got better. When I cut out alcohol, my spirit came back. An evolved life requires balance. Sometimes you have to cut one thing to find balance everywhere else."

~ Sarah Hepola

ABOUT THIS BOOK

Many people drink too much and don't realize the harm they can cause themselves and others. Some know they have a problem, but don't know how to solve it.

Alcohol misuse results in thousands of preventable deaths and hospitalizations every year from accidents, violence, and diseases including liver damage and cancer. The cost, in dollars alone, is truly staggering, estimated at billions per year. The price of heartache is incalculable. In New Zealand, and other Western cultures suicide is the leading cause of death, especially amongst our young people. Alcohol is a major contributing factor.

Alcohol, we are told, makes us happy. Very little is said about the side-effects—anxiety, depression, aggression.

Your Beautiful Mind: Control Alcohol & Love Life More provides an antidote by promoting a more mindful and responsible drinking culture.

It aims to help reverse the harm of alcohol. The goal is to normalize, not stigmatize sobriety. The agenda is to help you take back control, push back the booze barons' unbalanced and misleading ploys and restore the balance. The hope is that after reading this book, wellness will be the priority for all people regardless of circumstances and race.

It offers short, sound-bites of stand-alone readings designed to help you cultivate awareness and reexamine your relationship to alcohol amid the challenges of daily living.

Your Beautiful Mind: Control Alcohol & Love Life More offers a progressive program of holistic—mental, emotional, physical and spiritual—support, guiding you through essential concepts, themes, and practices on the path to sobriety, well-being, joy, and happiness.

The tone is gently humorous, sometimes challenging, occasionally provocative, but always compassionate and kind, and, I hope infinitely wise.

My aim is not to sound preachy or moralising, but to present information in such a way that you'll say: "I get it. I understand. There is another way." And then, when the booze barons try to tempt you again, you'll see through their ruse and no longer be tempted to imbibe their drugs.

All that I share are strategies that have worked for me personally through many of my own life challenges, and for my clients in my professional work as a holistic therapist, counsellor, and self-empowerment coach.

A central tenet of this book is to provide you with information and education that counteracts the dominant messages provided by booze barons whose purpose in life is to help you drink more. Of course, they want you to drink—their mission is to spin a grand profit. I also aim to share with you simple and powerful well-being strategies you can apply yourself—many from the comfort of your own home.

What you're about to discover may be eye-opening, mind-changing or rejuvenating reinforcement to follow through on what you already know.

The end goal? To make informed choices about what you are ingesting (ethanol and sugar), how much, and why—and to be empowered to change your relationship with alcohol once and forever.

Armed with the truth about alcohol you will gain:

- A new way to see and understand your relationship to alcohol
- The removal of the fear and stigma of admitting you need help
- Insight into the reasons why drinking too much is not your fault and that you have just become another cultural conditioning statistic
- Simple strategies to take back control

Your Beautiful Mind: Control Alcohol & Love Life More will strengthen your subconscious desire NOT to drink and help you make healthy, lasting, self-empowered change.

Experts suggest that it takes months, even years, of hardship to stop drinking. This book challenges this diagnosis and offers a different solution—and works...fast.

But at the end of the day, no one can make you control your drinking. You have to want to change. It is my hope that *Your Beautiful Mind* will strengthen your intention to quit or cut back drinking. The choice is yours, my friend.

Within this choice, is the chance to seek help, or not, for problems that keep you stuck, peer pressure that keeps you drinking, or traumas and open wounds that need healing—not numbing with alcohol.

I hope you will choose to free yourself from pain so that you may find the freedom, happiness, health, and joy you deserve and which awaits.

Your Beautiful Mind features the most essential and stirring passages from some of my previous books, exploring topics such as meditation, mindfulness, positive health behaviors, and touches on ways to working with fear, depression, anxiety, and other painful emotions.

Your Beautiful Mind: Control Alcohol & Love Life More expands upon these previous books and blends the latest scientific research, spotlights the cultural, social, and industry factors that support alcohol dependence, and also encourages a more holistic and mindful approach to the seriousness of life and the ever-present stressors we all face.

As one advance reviewer wrote to me before reading *Your Beautiful Mind*, "The people who I work with are wanting to eliminate alcohol from their lives and rebuild their lives, families, and relationships. They do not want permission, approval or instruction on how to drink mindfully."

However, after reading this book, he wrote, "I really like the approach that this book takes in not attempting to stop drinking totally. It instead explains and coaches how to manage and cope with consuming alcohol so that the damaging effects may be minimised. This is a very useful supportive book for 'drinkers' and their families."

The purpose of this book is not to trivialize, nor condone, legitimize, or sanction problem drinking. Being mindful doesn't mean being obstinately blind to the very real perils of alcohol abuse and addiction.

Being mindful is a call to awakening and purposeful action to build the life you want—free of addiction.

It's a willingness to consider the growing evidence that shows there is a different way—a lasting and empowering solution, and it's one you can master yourself.

Through the course of this book, you will learn practical, creative and simple methods for overcoming subconscious scripts that keep you craving alcohol, heightening awareness and overcoming habitual patterns and addictive behaviors that block happiness and joy and hold you back.

Brimming with a smorgasbord of easy-to-apply strategies that will boost your mental, emotional and physical well-being, *Your Beautiful Mind: Control Alcohol & Love Life More* is a timeless call to action for anyone who wants to cut back or quit drinking alcohol, get their life back and create a healthier, happier, joyful time on this planet.

Three Holistic Principles of Success

Your Beautiful Mind takes a holistic look at what it means, and what it takes, to control alcohol. Everything is interconnected: mind, body, and spirit. To succeed in your quest to control alcohol you'll need to unify and empower them all.

To avoid overwhelm and facilitate a selection of healing options I've sectioned *Your Beautiful Mind* into a cluster of principles. Principles aren't constricting rules unable to be shaped, but general and fundamental truths which may be used to help guide your choices.

Let's look briefly at The Three Principles of Sobriety and what each will cover:

Principle One, "The Call for Sobriety" will help you explore the truth about controlling alcohol and define sobriety on your own terms. You'll discover the rewards and 'realities' of becoming booze free, and intensify success-building beliefs. You may realize you have a problem, but many people don't. In this section, we'll look at definitions of what constitutes problem drinking—and what doesn't. We'll also explore the reasons you drink, the biology of emotions and how to get naturally high.

You'll learn some truths which powerful business would rather see hidden and clarify the huge costs alcohol imposes on all of us in **Principle Two, "Rethinking Drinking."** You'll also discover why love, anger, igniting the fire within, and heeding the call for self-empowerment is the cornerstone of future success.

Actions shout louder than words. **Principle Three: "Strategies for Sobriety,"** will help you take back control. You'll learn how to tame your subconscious mind, deal with stress, trauma, societal pressure, and other life-stuff that may drive you to drink.

Love will be your new drug of choice. Love for yourself, your significant others, and your life. Passion, purpose, joy—call it what you will—love is the cure for all our ills.

It sounds simple. And it is.

In this section of the book, you'll clarify and visualize what you really want to achieve. You'll then be better able to decide where best to invest your time and energy. You'll also begin exploring ways to develop your life and career in light of your passions and purposeful sobriety, maintain focus and bring your vision to successful reality.

Strategies to help you empower your spirit urge you to pay attention to the things that: feed your soul; awaken your curiosity; stir your imagination; and create passion in your life. You'll also discover how to strengthen your connection to your superconscious mind.

You may be surprised to discover that you have three minds, and more—you'll discover ways to empower them all to overcome obstacles, achieve greater balance and fulfillment and maximize your sobriety success.

Your health is your wealth yet it's often a neglected part of success. Techniques to help you heal and empower your body recognize the importance of a strong, flexible and healthy body to your mental, emotional, physical and spiritual success.

You'll be reminded of simple strategies which reinforce the importance of quality of breath, movement, nutrition, and sleep.

Avoiding burnout is also a huge factor in maintaining sobriety. When you do less and look after yourself more, you can and will achieve freedom from alcohol.

Throughout Your Beautiful Mind, you'll also boost your awareness of how surrounding yourself with your vibe tribe will fast-track your success, and when it's best to ditch your booze buddies or go it alone.

Even if you think you've got the alcohol thing licked or you don't believe you're addicted, find a sprinkling of inspiring people and discover their successful strategies to control their drinking or to quit.

Discovering some of the most successful ways people have overcome their dependence on alcohol or addiction to booze and achieved freedom for good will boost your belief in the fact that it's easy, simple, and within your control.

Where there's a will—there is a way.

You'll be inspired by others success. Importantly you'll learn how following your own truth will set you free.

HOW TO USE THIS BOOK

If you've been drinking too much, or just getting in your own way, you're in good company, many successful, talented, beautiful people have been there. I've been there too. Guess what, drinking too much and getting in your own way is, sadly, normal.

I promise there are solutions to the problems you're currently facing —and you'll find them in the pages that follow.

Dig into this book and let me, and other alcohol control experts, be your mentor, inspiration and guide as we call forth your passions, purpose, and potential.

Through the teachings of others, extensive research into alcohol recovery, the biology of desire and neurology of addiction and the mysteries of motivation, success, and fulfillment, *Your Beautiful Mind: Control Alcohol & Love Life More* will help you accelerate success.

Plus, I'll share a candid peek at my own personal experience, including many unsuccessful efforts to scale back my drinking—and how I found a strategy that was fun, fabulous and worked.

You'll also benefit from my experience and professional success with clients as a holistic therapist.

Together, we will guide you to where you need to go next and give you practical steps to control alcohol and find freedom and happiness.

Growing up I wasn't encouraged to drink less. My hope is that after reading *Your Beautiful Mind: Control Alcohol & Love Life More,* you will be!

Step into this ride joyfully and start creating your best life today.

- If you want to have more energy and fire in your belly
- If you want to have happy, healthy, loving relationships
- If you want to stress less and love life more
- If you want to improve your mental, emotional, physical and spiritual health...

Then *Your Beautiful Mind: Control Alcohol & Love Life More* is exactly the right the book for you—whoever you are, whatever challenges you are facing and however you define health, happiness, and sobriety.

The ideas described in this book apply to anyone who's trying to control alcohol and inject some purposeful sobriety into their life and work.

Your Concise Guide to Success

Your Beautiful Mind: Control Alcohol & Love Life More is a concise guide to controlling alcohol. My vision, like many of my other self-empowerment books, was simple: a few short, easy to digest tips for time-challenged, distraction-loaded, people who were looking for inspiration and practical strategies to encourage positive change.

In this era of information overload and distraction, I knew that people didn't need a large wad of words to feel inspired, gain clarity and be stimulated to take action.

In coaching and counseling sessions I'd encourage my clients to ask a question they would like answered. The questions could be specific, such as, 'How can I stop drinking?' Or vague, for example, 'What do I most need to know?' They were always amazed at how readily answers flowed.

The need for simple, life-affirming messages is so important. If you are looking for inspiration and practical tips, in short, sweet sound bites, this guide is for you.

Similarly, if you're a grazer, or someone more methodical, this guide will also work for you. Pick a section or page at random, or work through the tips sequentially. I encourage you to experiment, be open-minded and try new things. I promise you will achieve outstanding results.

Let experience be your teacher. Give your brain a well-needed break. Balance 'why' with how you feel and embrace how you feel or how you want to feel. Honor the messages from your intuition and follow your path with heart.

At the time of writing, I've just turned to the chapter, *Your Body Barometer*. It's a timely reminder that when you drink too much your mental, emotional and spiritual health can suffer.

The following remark from Coco Chanel may also speak to you: "I invented my life by taking for granted that everything I did not like would have an opposite, which I would like."

Your Caffeine Hit

As with my other wellness books, I encourage you to Think of *Your Beautiful Mind: Control Alcohol & Love Life More* as a shot of espresso.

Sometimes one quick hit is all it takes to energize your willpower, improve your mood, or kickstart your resolve.

But sometimes you need a few shots to sustain your energy. Or maybe you need a bigger motivational hit and then you're on your way.

You're in control of what you need and what works best for you. Go at your own pace but resist over-caffeinating. A little bit of guidance here and there can do as much to fast-track your success as consuming all the principles in one hit.

Skim to sections that are most relevant to you and return to familiar ground to reinforce home-truths. But most of all, exercise compassion and enjoy your experience.

Dive Deeper With *The Sobriety Journal: The Easy Way to Stop Drinking: The Effortless Path to Being Happy, Healthy and Motivated Without Alcohol*

Creating a Sobriety Journal was a major aid in my own recovery—you'll find some excerpts sprinkled throughout *Your Beautiful Mind: Control Alcohol,* and I've written a handy resource to help you create your own.

This guided book leaves you free to create your own bespoke journal tailored to support your needs. It includes, Journal Writing Prompts, Empowering and Inspirational Quotes and Recovery Exercises that can be of use in your daily journal writing, working with your sponsor or use in a recovery group.

Available in print and eBook at all good online retailers.

Your Beautiful Mind Workbook

Your Beautiful Mind: Control Alcohol & Love Life More print book will also be available as a workbook, with space to write your responses to the challenges and calls to action within the book.

Stress Less, Love You More & Create a Beautiful, Successful LifeToday!

PRINCIPLE ONE: THE CALL FOR SOBRIETY

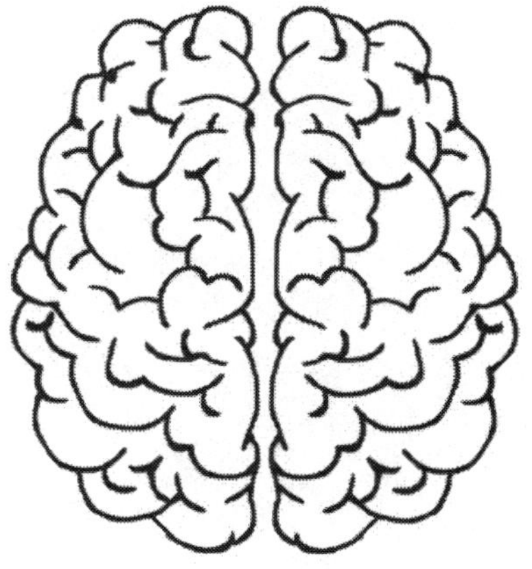

1

INTRODUCTION: THE TRUTH ABOUT SOBRIETY

Sobriety

Noun

1. the state or quality of being sober
2. temperance or moderation, especially in the use of alcoholic beverages
3. seriousness, gravity, or solemnity

"I THOUGHT you were going to tell me I couldn't drink at all," said my partner when I mentioned the title of this book.

Nope, sobriety does NOT mean abstinence. Although, some organizations like Alcoholics Anonymous define it that way. However, for a great many people abstinence is truly the only path to freedom.

Whether you're flirting with the idea of sobriety or starting out on your sober journey, you'll be glad to hear that sobriety, however you define it is about living life on your terms.

Your Beautiful Mind is not about telling anyone how much to drink or not to drink—the focus is on helping you make more informed decisions and empowered choices.

And, I'll be honest, my hope is that after reading this book you'll truly feel liberated. Liberated from the myth that committing to sobriety sentences you to a grey wasteland of boredom, devoid of pleasure and plagued with seriousness.

In fact, as you'll find the exact opposite. Sobriety is sexy, empowering, fun and smart. And you don't have to take it from me. Ask Jennifer Lopez, Colin Farrell, Russell Brand—me, and a whole bunch of other people who know life truly is more beautiful sober.

The truth about alcohol is that sobriety and abstinence have been given a bad rap. But the tide is turning as more and more people grow disenchanted with booze and the addiction of despair.

"Sobriety" is a word whose 12-step misuse now pervades our entire culture, along with ruining addiction treatment," says addiction expert Dr. Stanton Peele.

"In fact, the DSM psychiatric manual (unbeknownst to virtually everyone who uses it, including even experts who write about it) says Peele, contains no abstinence criterion for recovery (actually called remission)."

Sobriety is more than being a tee-total. It's more than fighting a daily battle with your willpower. It's more than the number of drinks you do, or don't knock back.

Sobriety actually means not drinking alcohol in excess, being intoxicated, or drunk. In the true context being sober means not being pissed, sobbing into your wine, puking your guts out, being a dickhead, a violent vermin or lying comatose in a gutter somewhere.

Ultimately, whether you opt for abstinence or moderation, controlling alcohol involves choice. The choice to drink, or not to drink.

"Yeah, right, you can control alcohol," a woman wrote in an alcohol forum when I shared the title of this book.

Granted, controlling alcohol, like controlling anything pervasive, takes concentrated, disciplined and motivated effort. Not only are you swimming against a tide of historical attitudes to alcohol that infect so many people today, but plenty of booze barons and associated industries gain eye-watering profits by persuasively encouraging you to drink more...and more...and more.

It seems as though everywhere you look somebody is trying to slip you another drink.

You're not even safe at home. The other day I received a delivery from BookDepository. Inside the package lay a bookmark advertising a staggering range of wines I could order online. And there I was thinking I had simply ordered a book. Nope, there is no escaping the onslaught.

But you can master the art of ignoring peoples' attempts to seduce you with their booze temptations and you can become a pro at zoning out.

It's incredibly liberating and empowering when armed with the truth about alcohol, you're no longer in its grip.

That's how it is for me, and it's how it can be for you. I started writing this book thinking I'd just scale back my drinking a weeny bit, but I discovered the life-changing magic of complete abstinence, not because I couldn't drink—but because I truly didn't want to.

And I'm betting that if you're willing to try my sobriety experiment you'll discover the surprising joy and life-changing benefits of abstinence.

Here are just a few:

- Better health

- More energy
- Greater enthusiasm for life
- Deeper and more fulfilling relationships
- Improved finances
- Deeper spiritual connection
- Enhanced creativity
- Elevated well-being,
- Peace of mind
- Freedom
- Happiness
- True joy
- Increased brainpower

....and so many more benefits we'll explore further in this book.

Be Empowered

Despite compelling evidence of both the considerable health risks of drinking alcohol, in many countries, including New Zealand, heavy or binge drinking, defined as having five or more drinks in one sitting at least once a month in the past year, has become the accepted norm.

Disturbingly, drinking to excess is actively encouraged as 'freedom of choice' and 'alcohol fuelled fun'.

Yes, you do have free choice. But if you're going to make better decisions, you'll need better information.

Interestingly, improving education is a tactic the New Zealand Police recently adopted. At least 30 underage drinkers, all aged between 14 and 17, were collared for breaching Wanaka's public liquor ban during the December 31 2017 public street party.

Instead of slapping them with a $250 instant fine, the police made them write essays about the impact of binge drinking on their teenage brains.

Worryingly, many said they got their alcohol from their parents—perhaps they too, should have been invited to put pen to paper. Increasing awareness is a key factor in changing any destructive habit.

Many people say they know they have a problem, they just don't know why they drink.We'll take a closer look at the diverse triggers that cause you to drink, why it's challenging to stop and how marketing moguls proactively feed your desire for their profitable vices.

The chapters in the section 'Rethinking Drinking' may be a sobering and timely reminder to cut back on the booze. You'll discover new knowledge, new choices, and discover how to get your fix from more positive addictions.

We'll also probe into the neurological causes of addiction. Once you understand the scientific, economic, cultural and systemic basis for your inexplicable behaviors and the truth about what alcohol does to your mind, body, soul, and relationships, you are unlikely to fall victim to addiction and alcohol abuse again. Even if it takes a few cycles of relapse to fully grasp the truth, you will be more empowered to fight back.

Best of all, once you've tasted life sober, mastered the art of living life raw, you'll be free. Life, even when crap happens, will be something you don't just survive, but joyfully, happily imbibe. You'll have mastered the art of living and the wisdom of no escape.

In the meantime, I encourage you to be a diagnostician—investigate alcohol in all its guises. Arm yourself with your own knowledge, don't just take it from me. And definitely, whatever you do, don't gain your knowledge from the booze barons. Seek impartial advice and be objective.

But first, let's test your knowledge. Then we'll take a look at the upside of drinking less. You'll be heartened to learn that quitting booze or reducing your daily quota is becoming cool. Sobriety, my friends, is the new drunk. You'll also discover, throughout this book, easy ways to get high naturally—swapping negative health-zapping addictions for positive life-affirming addictions—easily.

2

TEST YOUR KNOWLEDGE

"Drinking worked in the beginning: I felt wonderful, warm, and fuzzy... almost pretty...What I didn't know was that I was in a prison of my own making," says former addict Colette Baron-Reid—now a sober intuitive counselor & author.

If you're worried about your drinking or have had a heavy drinking problem for a while chances are you're well aware of the signifiant health implications, and how alcohol ruins many areas of your life.

But many people aren't. They binge drink like it's a sport, scull drinks like there's no tomorrow. Ignoring the wake of devastation they leave in their path, they resist making a change for the better. Sometimes they leave it until it's too late to undo their mistakes.

If you feel that it's time to rethink the role and purpose of alcohol in your life. Test your current knowledge by answering the questions below:

- Do you know what alcohol really is?
- How is alcohol made? What process creates stronger spirits?
- Is alcohol a known cause for more than 60 different health

conditions? Do you know what these are?

- Do you really understand the damage you're doing to your body when you're hung over?
- Why can a 5 percent beer can make you twice as drunk as a 4 percent version?
- What about an 8 percent craft beer? Is wine safer to drink than vodka?
- What is the definition of binge drinking? Can it kill you? Why can't you stop?
- Which country says it's fine to drink three pints a night?
- What is a unit of alcohol? What is a standard drink? Why does it matter?
- How many units of alcohol are deemed safe daily? Weekly? Why?
- Is it true that women should drink less than men?
- What are the health-effects and risk factors if you drink more than the recommended guidelines?
- Does alcohol depress the central nervous system at high doses?
- Did you know that alcohol can offer a short-term high, followed by deep lows, depression, anxiety and suicidal thoughts?
- Did you know that many alcoholic drinks include compounds called congeners that add to the taste, smell or color of the drink? Why do they increase the likelihood and intensity of suffering a hangover, and other undesirable side effects?
- Do you really know what the labelling on the bottles you buy really means?
- Do you know that lobbyists influence governments so they can maximise the sale of alcohol to minors, and society's most vulnerable people?
- Do you even care? Are you happy remaining blissfully blind?

You'll find the answer to these questions in the pages that follow.

3

ALCOHOL UNMASKED

Booze barons do such a great job of disguising alcohol that many people don't know what it really is.

Alcohol is ethanol, also known as ethyl alcohol or grain alcohol, and is a flammable, colorless chemical compound. Yes, folks, everything can really go up in flames when you drink.

I fondly remember Christmases spent at my grandmother's and the excitement we all felt when a match was held against the rum-soaked Christmas pudding and it burst into plumes of fire.

For some reason, until researching this chapter I never made the connection that booze was a flammable substance I poured down my throat.

Ethanol fuel is also used in some countries instead of gasoline in cars and other engines. In Brazil, for example, ethanol fuel made from sugar cane provides 18 percent of the country's fuel for cars.

In short, the alcohol or ethanol found in your favorite beer, wine, and spirits is a poison, masquerading as a happy drink. It's so toxic that, when consumed too quickly or in huge quantities, your body's default position is to expel it—usually in a totally unglamorous technicolor spray of vomit. That's if you're lucky.

Alcohol poisoning can, and does, cause death—both directly and indirectly through liver disease, breast cancer, and a staggering amount of other alcohol-related diseases. We'll explore the havoc caused by booze, as well as how sobriety leads to nirvana in the chapter, Health Havoc or Health Nirvana?

Yet, despite all the risks and dire health warnings, alcohol seems such a benign substance. Perhaps it's the allure of its origins—a uniquely natural process.

Alcohol is formed when oxygen deprived yeast ferments natural sugars found in fruits, grains, and other substances. For example, wine is made from the sugar in grapes, beer from the sugar in malted barley, cider from the sugar in apples, and most vodka from the sugar in fermented grains such as sorghum, corn, rice, rye or wheat (though you can also use potatoes, fruits or even just sugar.)

Many people use alcohol as a way to self-medicate their way through life's ups and downs. Peer into the history of alcohol and you'll find that its medical origins enjoy a good pedigree. Gin mixed with tonic containing quinine, for example, was historically used to treat malaria.

"So it's totally good for you," writes one enthusiastic supporter in an alcohol forum.

Yeah, if you've got malaria perhaps, but not if you're just sick and dog-tired of living.

Alcohol is classed as a 'sedative hypnotic' drug. That definition on its own may sound just like what you're craving until you discover the true impact. Sedative-hypnotic drugs depress the central nervous system (CNS) at high doses.

Hmmm, that doesn't sound so flash, especially if you're prone to knocking back a few too many drinks. Your central nervous system controls a majority holding of the key functions of your body and mind. The CNS consists of two parts: your brain and your spinal cord.

As you know, the brain is the chief conductor of your thoughts, interpreting your external environment, and coordinating body movement and function, both consciously and unconsciously. Complex functions, including how you think and feel, and maintaining homeostasis, a relatively stable balance between all the interdependent elements in your body, are directly attributable to different parts of your brain.

Your spinal cord with its network of sensitive nerves acts as a conduit for signals between the brain and the rest of the body.

You definitely don't want to mess with the way this important duo functions. But every time you ingest alcohol you do, weakening their ability to perform like virtuosos, interfering with maintaining a healthy balance and the finely tuned harmony which is so vital to your health, performance and effectiveness, and causing all systems in your body to play horribly off key.

Would you love to possess an outstanding ability in your field? Excel in your chosen profession? Tap into higher knowledge? Hone a much-loved or admired skill? Be universally admired? Many people think alcohol aids the fulfilment of these desires—until they realize their beliefs were deceptively wrong.

Sobriety on the other hand... now there's a different story.

At lower doses, alcohol can act as a stimulant inducing feelings of euphoria, optimism, and gregariousness. Everything looks beautiful, your belief in yourself, your talents, and your ability elevates like a seductive piece of music. Your inhibitions float away, suddenly you imagine yourself to be far better than you really feel. Shyness disappears, in its place talkativeness.

For a little while.

But pour more and more drinks down your throat, knock back liters of your favorite elixir and you'll quickly find yourself confronted by the truth. Alcohol is trouble.

Quite simply, alcohol knocks the life out of you. The more you drink, the higher the likelihood you'll become drowsy. Recall the drunk in the corner, slouched against the wall, or the once vivacious life of the party, barely able to hold her head in her hands, as she sits slumped at the bar. I've been there—it's a predictable rite of passage. In a culture that values drinking, this is normal.

Normal but definitely not glamorous, hip or cool.

But things get worse. Sometimes much, worse. Your breathing naturally slows into a state called respiratory depression. It can become exceedingly shallow or worse, stop entirely—what's truly frightening is you have absolutely no control. No one chooses to fall into an alcohol-fuelled coma, but this is exactly what happens to far too many people.

Very high levels of alcohol in the body can shut down critical areas of the brain that control breathing, heart rate, and body temperature, resulting in death. And, tragically, far too many beautiful people needlessly die this way.

Can I scare you sober? It's not my agenda, but I do know this—that's exactly what happened to Amy Winehouse. And it's exactly what's happened to a great many other talented, beautiful, smart people. People who only wanted to feel high, but never intended to die.

As well as its acute and potentially lethal sedative effects at high doses, alcohol undermines every organ in the body and these effects depend on your blood alcohol concentration (BAC) over time.

We'll examine the dangers of drinking both large and small alcoholic beverages over a short period of time in the chapter, Binge Drinking Blindness.

We'll also dive deeper into what constitutes safe drinking, including analyzing what constitutes a standard drink and why health authorities want you to control your drinking—assuming you don't want to kick the alcohol habit for good.

But first, let's stop to consider, how natural is alcohol really?

What's Hidden in Your Drink?

Ethanol made be created via a naturally occurring process, but that's not the end of the production cycle. The other thing to be mindful of is all the other hidden dangers lurking in your drinks.

Peer a little closer and you'll find all sorts of nasty additives—not to mention toxic sprays, pesticides, fungicides, chemical fertilizers and other things that infiltrate many crops. But you won't find many of these disclosed on the labels.

Sorry to spoil the party.

Health gurus cite dangerous levels of sulfites or sulphites (as it's spelled in New Zealand) and warn of harmful side-effects, particularly for those with a low tolerance.

The term sulfites is an inclusive term for sulfur dioxide (SO_2), a preservative that's widely used in winemaking (and most food industries) for its antioxidant and antibacterial properties. SO_2 plays an important role in preventing oxidization and maintaining a wine's freshness. When used in high levels, because it's considered harmful, it must legally be disclosed on product labels.

To be fair, many foods also contain sulfites. Some people claim the preservative is nothing to be alarmed by—unless of course, you include yourself in the numbers of people who are allergic. Sulfites cause bloating and itching in sulfite-sensitive people. Does your beloved have a beer gut or sulphite bloating?

Histamine High?

Some studies suggest sulfites and other additives, including compounds such as histamines and tannins, are connected to the pounding headaches many of us suffer after drinking. That, and our ballooning weight.

Fermented alcoholic beverages, especially wine, champagne, and beer are histamine-rich.

As the author and psychologist Doreen Virtue explains in her excellent book, *Don't Let Anything Dull Your Sparkle,* many people binge drink when stressed, but most don't realize that some of the excess weight may be attributed to stress-hormones and neurotransmitter responses. These biochemicals, Virtue says, are triggered by the fact when you're stressed you often binge on food and drinks to which you may unknowingly be allergic to, or which are intrinsically unhealthy.

As I've mentioned, any product that undergoes fermentation contains high levels of histamine. What I didn't know was that these histamines trigger allergic reactions in our body, especially if we're under a lot of stress.

Histamines get you both ways, not only occurring in the food and alcohol you drink, but also because when you're allergic to something your body releases its own histamine, says Virtue. "Stress produces histamine. We're all naturally allergic to stress," she says.

When you consume a diet that's high in histamine or histamine-inducing foods, your body becomes overwhelmed. Add a stressful lifestyle to the mix and it's no wonder you feel less than perky.

Histamines are also manufactured and released by our bodies not only when we're stressed but also when we're dehydrated. Again, alcohol, because it magnifies dehydration, makes things worse.

Virtue explains, "The trouble is that histamine produces uncomfortable symptoms such as bloating, itchy skin, profuse sweating, hot flashes, runny or stuffy nose, and feeling cold all the time, as well as low blood pressure, arrhythmia, anxiety, and depression."

Nice.

No wonder, we start to look and feel better when we lose the booze.

Other addictive beverages, like coffee and sugar-laden drinks also trigger histamine reactions. The net result is a 'histamine high.' This boosted energy and elation you experience is always short-lived and is always followed by an energy crash, plus other painful symptoms discussed above.

Before publishing her findings Virtue decided to test her theory and embark on a 30-day histamine-free diet.

"Within two days of going 'low-histamine,' I felt a youthful energy and exuberance that I had never experienced before. I felt well. I felt happy. And I knew it was due to the low-histamine diet... you cannot return to the old ways of bingeing upon histamine once you realize the process behind these binges."

Sugar Rush

Submerged in many alcoholic drinks are dangerous and highly addictive levels of sugar. Research collated in *New York Times* article stated, "Cravings induced by sugar are comparable to those induced by addictive drugs like cocaine and nicotine."

Latest research revealed in The New Zealand Listener in 2018 reveals the physiological and neurological reasons your brain makes you crave sugar. I share some of these findings in the chapter Sweet Misery. It's only since researching and writing this book that I realized I was more addicted to sugar than alcohol.

Whew! That's a relief. But it's also not—because both are tough habits to crack. Tough, but not impossible. Knowledge is power, right?

In summary, not only is alcohol a highly addictive poison, but your cravings, your weight gain, low energy levels and less-than-optimal mental and emotional health may be fuelled as much by additives and sugar, as it is ethanol or alcohol itself.

You can heal your life and it begins with examining the facts. Consider becoming an amateur sleuth and adopting the role of an investigative journalist. Discover how alcohol is made, including all the artificial things that are added to many products to make it tastier and more alluring—and potentially more dangerous to your health.

Perhaps this may be all the motivation you need to develop a healthy intolerance for alcohol.

4

SAVVY SOBRIETY

Many people struggle to control alcohol because they're not motivated by sobriety. But, being sober isn't just about not drinking.

Sobriety is achieved by putting energy and effort toward something you really desire.

Knowing *why* you want something is just as important as knowing *what* you want.

Why do you want to control your drinking? To feel better about yourself? To achieve wellbeing goals? Because you're afraid that your drinking it taking over your body and your life? To inspire others? Because you're curious that what you've been hearing is true—life really is better sober? Or something else?

We'll explore more ways to help you discover your driving purpose later in this book, but first here are just a few benefits of achieving sobriety:

- Improved mental health and wellbeing
- Better physical health
- Improved emotional health

- Elevated spiritual health
- Saves money
- Enriches your relationships
- Is an indispensable part of fulfilment
- Energizes you
- Liberates you
- Will change your life and the lives of those who matter most to you

Being sober sounds great, and it is. But the challenge is that so many of us have been brainwashed into believing it's awesome to be drunk. As I share later in this book, many of the people we look up to, including our political leaders have a dysfunctional relationship with alcohol—no wonder it's hard to implement laws aimed at reducing alcohol harm.

But if it's cool to be high, why do so many of us want to quit? Why do thousands of people sign on for Dry July or make New Year's resolutions to lose the booze only to be coerced or bullied into drinking again?

Giving up drinking can feel like losing your best friend, even your lover—until you remind yourself how alcohol is a fickle companion who lets you down again and again.

Sobriety, now there's a forever friend.

She won't turn sour, she won't piss you off, or get mad at you, and she won't rob you blind. Sobriety won't hijack your brain and make you say and do things you'll wildly regret in the wake of hangover hell.

Sobriety is not seedy or unpleasant. Sobriety is a sophisticated, serene, stabilizer in a world gone mad.

Sober

Synonyms

1. Not drunk
2. Thoughtful, steady, down-to-earth and level-headed
3. Serene, earnest
4. Not addicted

Who doesn't want a friend like that?

Sadly, the opposite is also true. Some of my best, most trusted friends turn into tyrants, either at the time of drinking or in the days that follow. These are just a few of the changes I notice when they drink alcohol:

- Overly critical
- Short-tempered
- Tyrannical
- Moody
- Solemn
- Angry
- Silent
- Withdrawn

Here's a short excerpt from my Sobriety Journal:

29 Dec 2016.

> *"A terrible, terrible evening. Me hiding in fear. Brett on a rampage. Smashing my fridge (taking it physically out of the studio and hurling it to the ground). 'Stress' brought on by the windows he shattered when he mowed the lawn, his frustration at the fountain not going, mowing the front paddock and returning, his eyes flaming and puffy.*
>
> *And then drinking. Three bottles of beer, then driving to the store and returning with a giant bottle of Mount Gay rum which he knows I hate him drinking. It always makes him so aggressive. He drinks it straight from the bottle. I feel panic rising in my chest. I feel real fear. I fear for my life.*

> *Smashed pots, plants, my canvases strewn with horrid words I cannot decipher.*
>
> *I'm cowering because I could quickly become a victim of his frenzied attack. I fear he has lost his mind. He* ***has*** *lost his mind. He has lost control.*
>
> *I really hate alcohol. I hate what it steals from me. Our love. Our dreams.*

Although this frightening, truly terrorizing episode happened so long ago, I still feel the fear. That's what traumatic episodes do to us—their linger in our body waiting to be triggered—or, with help, resolved. It's a chilling reminder, but also a motivating one, which fuels my commitment for sobriety, and my devotion to helping others free themselves from harm, save their relationships, regain their sanity—and so many of the other benefits sobriety promises and *delivers*.

Unlike alcohol, sobriety can be trusted.

Throughout this book I'll discuss some of my strategies for living in a booze soaked world, including how I keep my energy and vibration levels high and don't allow drunks to dull my sparkle.

One simple strategy I do find helpful, however, is to pin inspiring quotes somewhere visible to remind me to censure the tendency to demand others change or to judge.

Letting go of judgment creates peace, strength, and ultimately increases joy. Becoming judgment-free and leading by example is also one of the key sobriety steps recommended by many successful addiction programs. This includes self-judgment and self-criticism.

My current go-to quote is by Abraham Hicks, "Let others vibrate how they vibrate and want the best for them. Never mind how they're flowing to you. You concentrate on how you're flowing because one who is connected to the energy stream is more powerful, more influential than a million who are not."

You can see this quote, along with the image of a young woman in a glass jar, sending her loving light into the world. The jar represents the shield she places around herself, to protect her from negative people and dark outside forces.

I also invite love, not fear or anger to guide my day. I'm not saying it's easy—if it were the world would be a happier place. I work to remember how my loved ones are when they're sober—how kind they are, how caring. This love extends to me too. I know I'm a nicer, kinder person sober than I am drunk.

Exercising self-love, however, means accepting that sometimes there comes a time when being around people who abuse alcohol becomes too toxic. Their drinking may undermine your health, threaten your resolve, or cause you to constantly fear for your life. There are times you may have to quit not only the booze but people, places, and relationships that hold you back.

Finding joy in sobriety is a lifestyle choice—a very personal, and very empowered and empowering choice. It's a choice you make with eyes wide open, determined to celebrate and make the most of your one precious life in every way.

Humor, as you'll also discover, goes a long way.

This man is giving birth to a six-pack…'Father and beers are doing swell.'

It's a picture I drew in my Sobriety Journal, in part to remind me how staying sober improves my waistline.

> *Call it like it is....would you like a shot of ethanol and a gallon of sugar with that?*

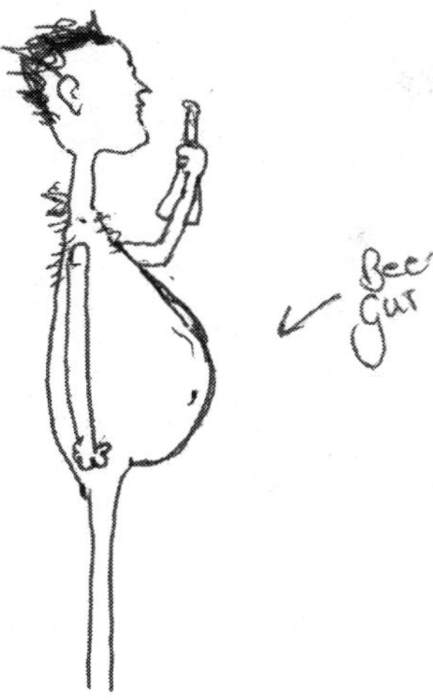
Bee
Gut

5

THE SURPRISING JOY OF SOBRIETY

Is it more fun to have one? The 'one-and-done' club is growing in popularity, despite considerable pressure to have more. Would you be happier? I know I am—'one or none', that's my new mantra. Rule number one, I never, ever drink when stressed.

Sobriety is my sunshine, my light, the sparkling clarity of a life infused with beauty. I love being sober. I love feeling in control.

Controlling alcohol has freed me from the darkness and despair that once stalked me, and which still haunts so many.

Sure, I no longer have the quick fix-magic potions to addle my brain, mask my fears, vanquish my insecurities. Making friends with social anxiety didn't come in a seductively beveled crystal flute fizzing with bubbles. Nope, it took a lot of hard graft.

But I have something more as a result. Heart-wide open I have my spirit, my soul, my self. I am supported, nourished, and free to be me —authentically, warts, vulnerabilities, flaws and all. And it feels great. And I never want to go back to the blindfolded darkness of short-term highs and long-term lows.

Self-love, self-compassion, self-acceptance, and self-care—they're all part of my toolkit. They're part of your tool-kit too.

What do they all have in common?

Loving you.

Loving you more than trying to fit in with your drinking buddies. Respecting and loving your body and soul so much that you no longer crave toxins. Delighting in the fact you're riding a wave of new enlightened consciousness.

The World is Sobering Up

It's heartening to see the savvy sobers enjoying increasingly good company. Globally there's an awakening and with it a rebirth, a renaissance of sorts. Being boozed is a relic from the dark ages and this is the era of enlightenment. Sobriety is queen, abstinence her cohort.

Magazines are running pieces about the 'sober-curious' movement. *Elle* is printing headlines such as 'Why I Decided to Break Up With Alcohol'. Others are talking about how toxic and deadly alcohol is to your skin. *The Huffington Post* is running with 'What Alcohol Really Does to Your Sex Life', and *Men's Health* is asking 'Why Drinking a Little Booze Each Day May be Killing You'.

"I don't drink or smoke or have caffeine," music diva Jennifer Lopez was reported as saying, in a women's magazine. "That really wrecks your skin as you get older."

Yep, not only is sobriety for savvy connoisseurs of health and well-being, but being booze-free is becoming a status symbol.

Sober is the new drunk.

Think Colin Farrell, Russell Brand and Duff McKagan, bass guitarist of Guns N' Roses, and one of the world's greatest rock musicians.

Sober and boring? I don't think so! Instead, they're admired, celebrated, held up as the new cool.

When I tell people I don't drink they look at me wide-eyed and full of awe. "Wow! I don't think I could function without a drink," many of them say. "I wish I could quit."

They can, you can—where there's a will, there is a way. Quite simply drinking alcohol is a habit, something many of us do without stopping to question why.

As the health risks become more and more apparent, and more valued, coupled with the unearthing of the tactical untruths peddled by suppliers, alcohol is going the way of cigarettes—on a fast-track trajectory out the door.

"I want to live. I don't want to die," UK songstress Adele famously declared when she shared her decision to considerably scale back her booze binging.

"I didn't want to live, but I didn't want to die," Colin Farrell once said before finding the courage and the will to quit drinking and seek help.

Your health is your wealth and sobriety will make you rich, a hundred times over. You'll find plenty of people investing in the new currency of sobriety.

Where once you couldn't party without a cigarette in your hand, or socialize without ingesting a plume of toxic smoke at a pub, booze-free bars, nightclubs and communities are sprouting like poppy seeds all around the world.

Having a Freaking Good Time Mindfully

"*No Beers, Who Cares* (BWC) isn't about making anyone feel bad about drinking. It's a movement towards shifting attitudes around how and why we drink and helping people become more aware of their beliefs and habits and having a freaking good time doing so," says Claire Robbie, the founder *No Beers, Who Cares.*

Robbie describes her *No Beers, Who Cares* initiative as not anti-alcohol, but as a pro-mindfulness initiative.

"There's a shift around the world as people understand how incredible life can be without drinking and it's time to bring that high vibration to New Zealand," Robbie says, "and it's an amazing step towards living more mindfully."

Claire Robbie was a news reporter on TV3's Nightline before a tumultuous time led her to discover the life-changing benefits of yoga and meditation and life without alcohol.

At a low point in her life, what started as a hobby became an essential part of her healing process, and as her love for her new practices grew, so did the awareness that she had discovered a new vocation.

"The focus is less about giving something up, but boosting your aware- ness of how much you gain," Robbie says.

Hack Your Habits Joyfully

"What we've seen is that giving up alcohol is a keystone habit. A keystone habit is one that unlocks your full well-being potential. Just a few of the benefits of going alcohol-free such as extra energy, motivation, vitality, productivity, money, and time, will begin to pave the way to the life you have always dreamed of," Robbie enthuses.

Whether you're tuning into *The Hello Sunday Morning* movement in Australia, *No Beers, Who Cares* in New Zealand, *Morning Gloryville* or *Off The Rocks* in the UK, or the ever-growing number of bars that have taken alcohol out of the mix, you'll find safety in numbers.

"When I first decided to undergo a long-term sober stint— total abstention from alcohol, for at least a few years and perhaps forever —I was full of dread, fear and feelings of deprivation, but after a while I realized how pivotal that decision was. It was only once I'd shelved alcohol that I was truly capable of sorting the rest of my life out. I then saw with absolute clarity how most people are addicted to something, and how the majority of those people are in denial about it," UK-based Jen Nelson, founder of Off The Rocks, says.

"I try not to waste time on regret, but if there's one thing I could go back and do differently, it would be to take a long and total break from alcohol a lot sooner than I did. Going sober for several years enabled me to identify the underlying causal reasons behind my once excessive drinking. Learning how to live sober also allowed me to cultivate proper coping techniques. I no longer celebrated every happiness with a drink and I stopped drowning my sorrows at the first sign of sadness. Recovery is so much more than giving something up, it's the way back to your authentic self."

How can you approach alcohol more mindfully? What might you be giving up by going alcohol free? How much might you gain? What are you prepared to change in your life? What would stop you?

Read on for further incentives on why sobriety is good for you, and why doing things to excess isn't just uncool but extremely dangerous —even fatal. Drink to excess, why would you? There comes a point in everyone's life when we decide, "I've had enough".

6

PROBLEM DRINKING?

"Not everyone who has a drinking problem will be able to see it," says recovering alcoholic and author of *Drink: The Intimate Relationship Between Women and Alcohol*, Anne Dowsett-Johnston.

Is your drinking already cause for concern? How do you know if you have a real problem, versus a temporary itch that you're using alcohol to scratch?

"If you want to know if you're getting into trouble, ask yourself ... are you drinking to numb? To numb feelings, to numb stress, to numb depression or anxiety?'" Dowsett Johnston says.

Alcohol makes us love life, we're told. If this is true, why aren't we a happier lot? Burnout, stress, anxiety have become worldwide epidemics—and with them alcohol and food addictions. We're either eating or drinking our way to happiness—or both.

Granted, not everyone has a problem with alcohol. Some people say there are four types of drinkers:

- Light or non
- Weekend-non binge

- Weekend drinkers who get drunk
- Heavy drinkers where every night is party night

The problem with those in the latter two categories may not be the booze, but maladaptive attempts to mask the causal factors.

Addictions and consistent alcohol abuse, in particular, are essentially attempts to escape pain. The nature and causal factors of this pain and the scale of dependency will vary in specifics and severity from person to person.

We all suffer painful experiences—but not everyone has learned to cope in a way that promotes, not depletes emotional, mental, physical and spiritual well-being, health and happiness.

Instead, too often developing and becoming dependent on unhealthy coping techniques becomes the norm—a norm that creates even more problems.

Fortunately, developing more positive ways of coping with life's inevitable ups and downs is not only possible but even enjoyable.

Changing your habits, even very deeply entrenched ones is a learned skill—and you'll find plenty of teachers when you go in search of answers.

Don't wait to hit rock bottom before you do something about your drinking or whatever's going on in your life that causes you to drink too much.

Start now. You can, and you will control your drinking. You don't always need to check in to rehab or pay mega dollars to sit on a psychologist's couch. It's totally fine if that turns out to be your sobriety solution, in full or in part.

The trouble with the 'disempowered' and 'disease' model of addiction, is that a great number of people can lead you to believe that controlling alcohol is completely beyond your reach.

Being told that if you drink too much, you have a disease, an incurable one at that, is neither helpful, truthful, nor empowering—even if it does feel better to know that it's not your fault that you drink too much.

We'll discuss the escalating rise of the disease model of addiction later in this book, but let's look at how some of the pros define addiction and substances abuse—what they focus on and what they miss.

The Maladaptive Pattern of Relying on Alcohol

Psychologists, psychiatrists, and many other addiction specialists predominantly focus on addiction as being a mental disorder, rather than an attempt to self-medicate or anaesthetize ones way through life. Very often a person's personal history of trauma, bullying or societal factors which aid, abet and accelerate their drinking are ignored.

The primary source used to classify problem drinking is provided by the American Psychiatric Association and their Diagnostic and Statistical Manual of Mental Disorders known as the DSM

Over-consuming alcohol is a disease we're told. A disorder of the mind, or an inherited genetic defect. DSM followers turn a blind eye to the fact that alcohol is a self-prescribed, self-served, legalized drug of choice turned to by many as their stress, anxiety, depression, trauma or grief-numbing cure.

Granted, not a particularly robust one, but perhaps, not the 'only-able- to-be-cured-by-medical-professionals' illness we have been led to believe.

"There's an enormous sense of self-medication.... The fastest thing you can do at the cutting board is open a bottle of wine, pour yourself a glass. It's faster than going to your doctor to say 'I'm suffering from burnout,' it's faster than going to a yoga class and relaxing in a different way," says Dowsett-Johnston.

Even though Johnston knew she was getting into trouble with her drinking she says, "It took two family members and a sweetheart who confronted me, and luckily I took a sledgehammer and went to rehab and I'm in my 10th year of sobriety."

As you'll discover later in this chapter, with the passing of time alcohol has shifted from being viewed as a problem of faulty, or maladaptive behavior, to one of disease.

This has opened the route to funding, and the creation of profitable business lines by drug companies scrambling to cure the 'disease' (or what I call the dis-ease) created by the world's most popular and legalized drug.

As a result, they have created a range of pharmaceuticals and manufactured drugs promising the ultimate (and profitable) cure. I recently heard they are trying to create an alcohol vaccine. Really? When did loving alcohol too much, or using it as an upper or a sedative, equate with Swine Flu, Chicken Pox, or Aids for that matter?

What if the ultimate cure lies in your own hands—a more mindful, holistic and therapeutic approach to how much you drink and why.

We're told loving alcohol too much is something we can't cure ourselves—that total abstinence is the only remedy. In my professional and personal experience, very often people choose to quit alcohol for good because they're just so over it.

Once alcohol is unmasked for the troublemaker it is, like a shitty lover, people choose never to go back. Whether it's fear of the havoc booze creates, or love—the joy and bliss they discover in their new partnership with life being alcohol-free—people who choose abstinence know life is better, way better, sober.

"You know, I never thought I'd never drink. I loved it, but going sober has forced me to face up to who I really am. I don't always have to be the life of the party. I can just leave and it's okay. So, I've realised I'm a lot more serious than I pretended to be," said the 36-year-old Hayley Holt, former ballroom dancing queen, snowboarding legend and TV star, and the former girlfriend of ex-All Black Captain, Richie McCaw, once said.

So serious in fact in 2017 she turned her set her sober sights high and turned her focus toward Parliament and campaigned in the electorate held by former Prime Minister, Sir John Key, on behalf of The Green Party.

Actor Colin Farrell also testifies that once problem drinking is kicked not only is life infinitely better—*you* are better.

"I have yet to meet a person whose sobriety has made their life worse. I have yet to. But I am open to it. If you find someone please get in touch with me because I would love to have a chat with them and ask them a couple of questions. I have yet to meet a person whose sobriety didn't make a better father, a better friend..."

Kristin Davis, most famous for her role as Charlotte York Goldenblatt in *Sex and the City*, has been alcohol-free since 1987. "Sometimes it would be nice to just have some red wine with dinner, but it's not worth the risk. I have a great life, a great situation. Why would I want risk self-destructive behavior?"

What do these people and others have in common?Their drinking was a problem—until it wasn't.

The chances are that you don't need a book and checklists to tell you that you have a problem, but just in case you're amongst the group of people who truly don't know how out of hand your drinking is getting you may be interested to learn what the American Psychiatric Association (APA) classifies as problematic.

What is Problem Drinking?

Regardless of whether you side with alcohol being or not being a disease, the APA classifications of problem drinking include:

- Tolerance and the never decreasing requirement for more

- Withdrawal symptoms when you can't get your fix
- Difficulty in giving up
- Persistent physical, psychological, social, mental and emotional problems that are likely to have been caused or exacerbated by your alcohol

The more symptoms you have, the more urgent the need for change.

Mmmm, using this definition, it would appear 85 percent of the drinking population has a problem. Remember this when people try to shame you for not drinking with taunts such as, "Do you have a problem?" No, my friend, they have the problem.

Addiction (termed substance dependence by the American Psychiatric Association—APA) was once defined as, "a maladaptive pattern of substance use leading to clinically significant impairment or distress."

This maladaptive pattern manifests by three (or more) of the following, occurring any time in the same 12-month period, say the APA:

1. Tolerance, as defined by either of the following: (a) A need for markedly increased amounts of the substance to achieve intoxication or the desired effect or (b) Markedly diminished effect with continued use of the same amount of the substance.

2. Withdrawal, as manifested by either of the following:

(a) The characteristic withdrawal syndrome for the substance, or

(b) The same (or closely related) substance is taken to relieve or avoid withdrawal symptoms.

3. The substance is often taken in larger amounts or over a longer period than intended.

4. There is a persistent desire or unsuccessful efforts to cut down or control substance use.

5. A great deal of time is spent in activities necessary to obtain the substance, use the substance, or recover from its effects.

6. Important social, occupational, or recreational activities are given up or reduced because of substance use.

7. The substance use is continued despite knowledge of having a persistent physical or psychological problem that is likely to have been caused or exacerbated by the substance (for example, current cocaine use despite recognition of cocaine-induced depression or continued drinking despite recognition that an ulcer was made worse by alcohol consumption).

> **"We just liked to have a good time."**

CAN you tick-off three or more of the above? I bet you never thought of yourself as being maladaptive. As the founder of *Soberly*, a movement dedicated to supporting sober warriors, Libby Wallace writes,

"I remember a lecture I went to for one of my psychology papers, around 9 years ago, and the lecturer stood at the front and did a 'drinking quiz' similar to the Ministry of Health one to find out whether or not you have a drinking problem. About 60 out of the 100 students put their hands up to say that they had rated themselves with a score that effectively meant they were an alcoholic. After discussing with a few friends after, and in the tutorial later, we thought it was funny and that because we were students, it didn't relate to us, we just liked to have a good time."

Alcohol Use Disorder & The Disease of Alcohol

In 2000 the DSM-IV criteria for substance dependence included several specifiers, one of which outlines whether substance dependence is accompanied by physiological dependence (evidence of tolerance or withdrawal) or without physiological dependence (no evidence of tolerance or withdrawal).

In addition, remission categories are classified into four subtypes: (1) full, (2) early partial, (3) sustained, and (4) sustained partial; on the basis of whether any of the criteria for abuse or dependence have been met and over what time frame.

The remission category can also be used for patients receiving agonist therapy (such as methadone maintenance or drugs designed to control alcohol dependence) or for those living in a controlled, drug-free environment.

This definition was altered in the 5th edition of the DSM. As compared to DSM-IV, the DSM-5's chapter on addictions was changed from "Substance-Related Disorders" to "Substance-Related and Addictive Disorders" to reflect developing understandings regarding addictions.

The DSM-5 specifically lists nine types of substance addictions within this category (alcohol; caffeine; cannabis; hallucinogens; inhalants; opioids; sedatives, hypnotics, and anxiolytics; stimulants; and tobacco).

These disorders are presented in separate sections, but they are not fully distinct because all drugs taken in excess activate the brain's reward circuitry, and their co-occurrence is common.

Problem drinking that becomes severe is given the medical diagnosis of "alcohol use disorder" or AUD in the DSM-V and is defined in the DSM-5 as a chronic relapsing brain disease characterized by compulsive alcohol use, loss of control over alcohol intake, and a negative emotional state when not using. An estimated 16 million people in the United States have AUD. Approximately 6.2 percent or 15.1 million adults in the United States ages 18 and older had AUD in 2015. This includes 9.8 million men and 5.3 million women. Adolescents can be diagnosed with AUD as well, and in 2015, an estimated 623,000 adolescents ages 12–17 had AUD.

To be diagnosed with AUD, individuals must meet certain criteria outlined in the Diagnostic and Statistical Manual of Mental Disorders (DSM). Under DSM–5, the current version of the DSM, anyone meeting **any two of the 11 criteria during the same 12-month period receives a diagnosis of AUD.**The severity of AUD—mild, moderate, or severe—is based on the number of criteria met.

How Do You Measure Up?

To assess whether you or loved one may have AUD, here are some questions to ask. In the past year, have you:

- Had times when you ended up drinking more, or longer than you intended?
- More than once wanted to cut down or stop drinking, or tried to, but couldn't?
- Spent a lot of time drinking? Or being sick or getting over the after effects?
- Experienced craving—a strong need, or urge, to drink?
- Found that drinking—or being sick from drinking—often interfered with taking care of your home or family? Or caused job troubles? Or school problems?
- Continued to drink even though it was causing trouble with your family or friends?
- Given up or cut back on activities that were important or interesting to you, or gave you pleasure, in order to drink?
- More than once gotten into situations while or after drinking that increased your chances of getting hurt (such as driving, swimming, using machinery, walking in a dangerous area, or having unsafe sex)?
- Continued to drink even though it was making you feel depressed or anxious or adding to another health problem? Or after having had a memory blackout?
- Had to drink much more than you once did to get the effect

you want? Or found that your usual number of drinks had much less effect than before?

- Found that when the effects of alcohol were wearing off, you had withdrawal symptoms, such as trouble sleeping, shakiness, irritability, anxiety, depression, restlessness, nausea, or sweating? Or sensed things that were not there?

Remember that meeting any two of the 11 criteria during the same 12-month period means you receive a diagnosis of AUD.

If you have any of these symptoms, your drinking may already be a cause for concern. The more symptoms you have, the more urgent the need for change," say professionals. But you know this already—or you wouldn't be reading this book.

Remember, there is no shame in admitting you have a problem. You're in good, or is that poor company? You decide. The true tragedy is not the problem, but not seeking help.

Like cocaine and heroin, shopping for things we don't need or eating sweet sugary food is addictive and satisfies our brain's craving for dopamine until we get our next fix.

Marketing moguls have known this for a long time and target people indiscriminately. Everywhere you look you're bombarded with ads about alcohol and sugar fixes that will cure our blues and make us supposedly happier and healthier.

Even the stuff dangled as healthier often has something to hide. Loaded with essential nutrients, natural flavors? Or concealing more than double your daily sugar requirement.

It's time to get wise!

Forget about waiting for law changes, forget about lobbying governments for more enlightened regulations. Take back your power. Open your eyes. It's not easy to change but you can begin by asking yourself more empowering questions, such as:

- Do I really need that fix?
- Will it impact on my wellbeing? How?
- How does alcohol work? Can I find a healthier, cheaper, more effective way to feel better?

The answers may prove illuminating. You may discover, as I have, that a swim in the ocean, a soak in the local hot mineral pools, a night at the movies, a massage, twenty-minutes mediation, or diverting the money I'm saving by not drinking booze for treats like pedicures, delivers a far faster, friendlier fix.

7

WOUNDED WARRIORS

If you're struggling with alcohol abuse or you're using booze to self-medicate, this doesn't necessarily make you an alcoholic—this doesn't mean you have a disorder or an incurable disease.

Self-medicating or anaesthetizing yourself with booze doesn't make you hopeless. But it does create an exponential increase that unless you become aware of how much you drink, why you drink and learn how to take back control, you'll continue to over-drink.

A great many people drink alcohol to mask or numb the symptoms of their wounds.

No one escapes walking in this world without some degree of hurt. For many people this hurt is profoundly deep.

The first cuts, experts (and songwriters) say are the deepest—very often these wounds are inflicted during childhood.

Tragically, what should be a happy time of innocence is one of incalculable pain. Incest, rape, physical abuse, emotional neglect—and many more horrid crimes, including murder, are often committed under the influence of alcohol.

Our local tavern, a sports and gambling bar, proudly tells patrons that they can bring their families, yet some 20 metres or so down the road a community noticeboard warns, "Kids are safer when you are sober. Ease up on the drink."

Tragically, it's a message that falls on far too many ears too deaf to hear, eyes too blind, and minds too inebriated to see the truth about alcohol.

Almost no-one escapes the toll of alcohol. Neither money, nor affluence, nor sobriety, nor age escapes its wrath. As I share in the opening of this book, my grandmother was four, and her brother aged six, and were outside the pub when their alcoholic father got into a drunken-brawl and murdered a man. Molly and her brother were forced apart—her brother was adopted and my grandmother spent her childhood being bounced out of foster homes. They never saw each other, or their parents, again.

Walking wounded? You bet. My grandmother spent her life seeking comfort from alcohol, even a stint in rehab couldn't dislodge the habit. Her brother, in adulthood, took his life.

Neither of them was ever offered help to heal the wounds of their past.

In *The Biology of Desire: why addiction is not a disease*, Marc Lewis shares the following testimony from an addiction counselor and former alcoholic,

"I have had a long hard look inside about how I feel personally about addiction. I do not feel that I have or had a disease. I see my past drinking as a behavioral problem, a learned response to dealing (or not dealing) with emotional pain and stress. Once I achieved the excavating of my wounds I no longer lived with the same anxiety or sense of dread/guilt and shame."

Personally, I have always been troubled by the preference of mainstream psychology to categorize and pathologize unwellness without delving deeper into its origins.

Instead, wounds are plastered over—seemly *cured* by a steady diet of pills and prescriptions. It was refreshing to read Lewis's book and this account. I encourage you to purchase a copy of his book. It's a brilliant exposé on the truth of addiction and the road to recovery.

Yes, I am overjoyed to say, times are slowly changing. *Slowly.* Unwellness is still a multi-billion dollar industry—there are powerful incentives to keep people dependent on the promise that the latest drug will cure.

Yet there is also an explosion of interest in alternative approaches to health and well-being and with it, the treatment of addiction. Three modern-day factors appear to herald the call for change:

- The escalating epidemic of depression, stress, anxiety and addiction
- The failure of the pharmaceutical industry to come up with sustainable solutions—let alone side-effect-free cures
- A flurry of reputable scientific studies validating the impact of therapies, once devalued and demoted as 'alternative'.

Transcendental meditation, prayer, massage, diet and a wide array of healing modalities, including energy healing, are on the ascent. Science it seems, has finally validated what many ancient cultures have always known—mind, body, spirit and environment are interconnected.

People are waking to the real reasons they drink.

As Legendary rock star Alice Cooper said in an interview, "I didn't realize that I was an alcoholic until I realized that alcohol was not for fun anymore. It was medicine."

You may, Cooper and others, may identify with the label 'alcoholic.' You may find it empowers you, like finally being given a diagnosis that explains the symptoms of illness that has made you sick for so long.

"I feel better now that I know what it is," so many people say when told that what ails them has a name. But labels can be limiting. Labels can pathologize, categorize, and demoralize. What purpose does it serve to be labeled an alcoholic? What solution does it bring? Perhaps it helps fuel your will. Fantastic. But it just seems like a negative affirmation that feels bad.

Why not say, as I do when offered alcohol, "I don't drink." When people ask, "why not?" I smile and say, "I like it too much."

Rather than spend time on carefully manicured labels consider diving deeper and bringing to light the wounds or triggers that drive you to drink. Consider exorcizing the trauma that has severed your growth, stolen your childhood, blocked your joy and kept you stuck in a cycle of abuse.

Seek help.

- Seek help to heal the wounds of the past
- Seek help to free you from a toxic relationship
- Seek help to liberate you from untenable job stress
- Seek help from whatever or whoever causes you to over-drink.

Perhaps you don't drink to plaster over traumatic wounds. Perhaps your drinking habit is your quick-fix strategy to take the sharp edge off living in this world.

Whatever your reasons, whatever your motivations, whatever has attracted you to this book, it's my sincerest hope that you find encouragement, help, and healing in the pages that follow.

I'd like to encourage you to view this book as Home Rehab—your in-house holistic addiction recovery center.

Instead of forking out thousands of dollars to be treated by some of the world's most esteemed addiction specialists you'll find some of the best of the best in the pages that follow including:

- A diet of knowledge and education
- The latest developments in mind and body science, including neurotheology, neuroesthetics, psychotherapy and more
- Mind, body, and soul therapies—including energy psychology and holistic healing—including meditation

The Path to Sobriety

I promise to break down the path to sobriety in ways you can easily understand and apply to your own life.

Knowledge is power. Ultimately long-term success in winning the war on alcohol can be explained through medical science and psychology— and marketing...how the booze barons encourage you to act against your best interests.

Understanding alcohol from all angles will offer substantive reasons for why it works.

Importantly, what I'd love you to take away from reading this book is that there is no one path to sobriety. You may or may not be able to go it alone, you may need help, you may need therapy, but regardless of the approach you take, controlling alcohol is a long-term lifestyle change.

Very often, as I've said, it may mean spotlighting and healing the wounds of your past.

Comedian and former addict Russel Brand shares his story of childhood sexual abuse in his book *Recovery: Freedom From Our Addictions.* In his book he reinterprets The Twelve Step recovery process and champions the call for abstinence.

Similarly, Duff McKagan, the former bass guitarist of Guns N' Roses and one of the world's greatest rock musicians, shares how he used alcohol to self-medicate his agonizing anxiety. The origin of his pain he says, stemmed from being asked to lie to his mother about his father's affairs, their subsequent divorce and his father's own heavy drinking.

McKagan devised his own program of anxiety treatment and alcohol recovery. Read the inspiring story of a man who partied so hard he nearly died, in his book *It's so Easy and Other Lies.*

Anne Dowsett Johnson, a journalist and self-described recovering alcoholic, and the daughter of an alcoholic herself, urges us all to wake up to the wilful blindness to the damages of drinking in our culture, and explores disturbing trends and false promises peddled by alcohol barons in her book *Drink: The Intimate Relationship Between Women and Alcohol.* For Dowsett, medical intervention through prescribed anti-depressants played an instrumental role in her recovery.

AA's 12-step approach didn't work for stressed entrepreneur Russ Parry. But years of therapy, couple counseling , renewing his faith and a program of recovery offered by his church did—alongside changing his relationship to work. He shares his journey to abstinence in his book, *The Sober Entrepreneur.*

These are just some of the many people and books I have come to admire as I embarked on my own journey to understand why I drank so much and why I couldn't stop.

For these people, sharing their stories was part of their healing process—that and the desire to pay-it-forward. In my book, E*mploy Yourself* from my bestselling *Mid-Life Career Rescue* series, I share how health coach Sheree Clark numbed her job blues by over-drinking until she realized booze was never going to be a long-term sustainable solution.

She sold her business and created a new career as a healthy living coach. She still enjoys a drink—but says since her career change that she couldn't be happier or healthier.

As author and filmmaker Michael Moore said, "I want us all to face our fears and stop behaving like our goal in life is merely to survive. Surviving is for game show contestants stranded in the jungle or on a desert island. You are not stranded. Use your power. You deserve better."

I took these words to heart many years ago. Anxiety and depression run in my family—as does a tendency to place a stop-cap on dreams. As you've read, my grandmother grew up in foster care, plagued by the shame of her family secret—her father was murdered a man. It doesn't matter that he was drunk, that he only meant to land a punch. Murder is murder, right? At least it is to those quick to judge.

I'm sure that Molly's painful upbringing had an impact on how much she drank. She was such a beautiful women with so much truly tragic trauma, including the death of her first child—a much-longed for son who arrived into the world still-born.

My grandmother's upbringing also impacted my mother and her sister. My mom told me that she couldn't recall ever coming home from school without finding her mother in bed. My grandmother's emotional distance and attempts to numb her pain, in turn, impacted my mom's ability to give me the love I craved as a child.

My dad suffered the trauma of emotional neglect too. He was dumped in a boarding school when he was only four—supposedly for his highest good. He never knew his father, and only found out when he was in his 70s that he had a sister. Growing up, he never experienced a hug or knew true affection.

I understand now why, growing up, I, nor my siblings were ever hugged. We still don't. Hugging feels awkward, stiff, painful—foreign.

Like Amy Winehouse and so many others with wounded childhoods, early traumas can leave permanent scars that alcohol and other drugs appear to smooth.

Writing this book has awakened many painful memories, I found myself grieving for the feeling of belonging I never felt. But writing and time has healed these memories too—knowledge, truth, love and acceptance does that.

I've worked hard to overcome the wounds of my childhood—my adulthood too.

You should, too. Your past doesn't need to stop you.

"A lot of people feel like they're victims in life, and they'll often point to past events, perhaps growing up with an abusive parent or in a dysfunctional family," writes Rhonda Byrne in *The Secret*.

"Most psychologists believe that about 85 percent of families are dysfunctional, so all of a sudden you're not so unique. My parents were alcoholics. My dad abused me. My mother divorced him when I was six... I mean, that's almost everybody's story in some form or not," she says.

The author of the *Chicken Soup For The Soul* series, Jack Canfield, also speaks to this point: "The real question is, what are you going to do now? What do you choose now? Because you can either keep focusing on that, or you can focus on what you want. And when people start focusing on what they want, what they don't want falls away, and what they want expands, and the other part disappears."

In hindsight, you will see your life experiences as a gift. As Isabel Allende once said, "Without my unhappy childhood and dysfunctional family, what would I have to write about?"

I channel my life experiences into my books. I pay it forward and share how I learned to empower my mind, body, and soul. I studied Buddhist philosophy. I learned Transcendental and mindfulness meditation—and praise the life-altering magic of this beautiful tool as often as I can.

Something, fashion designer, Stellar McCartney has also done recently, when in a 2018 article she revealed how in her twenties she turned to meditation after her mother's death. "Transcendental Meditation keeps me sane," McCartney says.

At the time of writing she is 46, and wants everyone to have the chance to reap the same benefits, whether they have a raw emotional need for TM, like she did, or not. Which is why, despite her preference to keep her private life away from the spotlight, she gave her first interview on meditation.

Reading her account, and those of others, fortifies my own spiritual and wellbeing practices. As does reading self-empowerment and personal development books.

When I was struggling with my own anxiety and depression I devoured nearly every self-help book on the planet—and beyond. I went to healers and sought counseling.

I trained to be a hypnotherapist, counselor, and therapist, and gained other healing skills. I continue to pass on the knowledge I've learned to my clients and readers like you to help empower us all to live our best lives. It's a large part of the motivation behind sharing so much of my own personal story and vulnerabilities in *Your Beautiful Mind*. This is me 'unplugged.'

Every day I fight for my dreams.

We all enter this life, and leave it, with different challenges. Different parents, siblings, life experiences. The pain of your past doesn't need to define you. If you are prepared to be honest and vulnerable and to do the graft, you know what you need to do to empower your life and your work.

Throughout this book we'll explore a diverse range of strategies to help you either ease up on the drink or ditch it entirely. For some people, when they lose the triggers that drive their craving, control comes easily.

For others, alcohol is a serious and dangerously addictive substance—they come to accept that they just can't handle it.

Whatever camp you're in, you are the expert in your own life. You are not powerless to make a change for the better. Empowering yourself is the biggest, most vital, most life-affirming skill of all.

As former addict and leading neuroscientist Marc Lewis writes in this book, *The Biology of Desire: why addiction is not a disease,* alcoholism and addiction "can spring up in anyone's backyard. It attacks our politicians, our entertainers, our relatives, and often ourselves. It's become ubiquitous, expectable, like air pollution and cancer."

Shaming, blaming and naming is not the cure, compassion understanding, and living life on your terms is.

As Lewis also notes, "Many experts highlight the value of empowerment for overcoming addiction. In fact, most former addicts claim that empowerment, not powerlessness, was essential to them, especially in the latter stages of their recovery. Sensitivity to the meaning of empowerment in recovery may be greatest for those who've been disempowered in their social world, including women, minorities, the poor, and those with devastating family histories."

Abusing alcohol is not a disease. It's a coping strategy—one, before reading this book, you may not have been aware of.

As you read this book, you'll reclaim your power and decide whether alcohol has anything positive to contribute to your life at all, or whether you'd be better off putting your money, your energy, your time, your happiness and your health into something, or someone, who's a less abusive lover. Yes, you will decide—it's that simple, and at times, that difficult.

Throughout *Your Beautiful Mind: Control Alcohol,* we'll explore ways to heal the past and exorcize unhelpful emotions that keep you stuck in a cycle of destructive feelings.

As Candace Pert writes in, *Everything You Need to Know to Feel Go(o)d,*

"Buried, painful emotions from the past make up what some psychologists and healers call a person's 'core emotional trauma'.

"The point of therapy—including bodywork, some kinds of chiropractic, and energy medicine—is to gently bring that wound to gradual awareness so it can be re-experienced and understood.

"Only then is choice possible, a faculty of your frontal cortex, allowing you to reintegrate any disowned parts of yourself; let go of old traumatic patterns, and become healed, or whole."

Lets take a deeper dive into how to control alcohol before it seizes the throttle and controls you.

Did you enjoy this excerpt?

ALSO BY CASSANDRA GAISFORD

Mid-Life Career Rescue: The Call for Change

Take the stress out of making a change, confirm your best-fit career and move toward your preferred future.

Available in print and eBook from online retailers.

Mid-Life Career Rescue: What Makes You Happy

Clarify what makes you happy and find your point of brilliance.

Available in print and eBook from online retailers.

Mid-Life Career Rescue: Employ Yourself

Start a business on the side while holding down your job. Or take the leap to self-employed bliss. Choose and grow your own business with confidence. This handy resource will show you how.

Available in print and eBook from online retailers.

Mid-Life Career Rescue-3 Book Bundle-

Box Set (Books 1-3): The Call for Change, What Makes You Happy, Employ Yourself

More passion, less career groundhog day! Fast-track your success and instantly save $$$ when you buy this bundle of 3 eBook best-sellers.

Available in print and eBook from online retailers.

How to Find Your Passion and Purpose: Four Easy Steps to Discover A Job You Want and Live the Life You Love

Focus your energy and time to achieve outstanding personal and professional results. Find your point of brilliance and purpose in life.

Available in print and eBook from online retailers.

How to Find Your Passion and Purpose Companion Workbook

Hands on help to guide and support you **in practical, easy-to-understand steps.**

The Passion Journal:

The Effortless Path to Manifesting Your Love, Life, and Career Goals

Would you love to attract your soul mate but have no idea what to do or how to begin? Would you love to change careers, or are you thinking of starting a business? Could your health do with an overhaul, or do your finances need rescuing? This ultimate guide contains the best practices of creating the life you deserve and manifesting a prosperous life easily.

Available in print and eBook from online retailers.

The Passion-Driven Business Planning Journal:

The Effortless Path to Manifesting Your Business and Career Goals

Are you thinking of starting a business? Would you love to employ yourself but have no idea what to do or how to begin? Or do you have an existing business but yearn for a fresh start? First things first: start from your heart. Your passion-driven business planning journal is the perfect place to begin your love affair.

Available in print and eBook from online retailers.

Boost Your Self-Esteem and Confidence

Be empowered! Heed the call for greater significance—six easy steps to increase self-confidence, self-esteem, self-value and love yourself more

Available in print and eBook from online retailers.

The Art of Success: Leonardo da Vinci

The 8-Step Blueprint to True Success for Your Relationships, Your Bank

Account, Your Body and Your Soul

Leonardo da Vinci had to overcome obstacles to succeed just like you and I. Be inspired by his blueprint for success.

Available in print and eBook from online retailers.

The Art of Success: Coco Chanel

The 8-Step Blueprint to True Success for Your Relationships, Your Bank Account, Your Body and Your Soul

Coco Chanel didn't let poverty, rejection, abandonment and fear stop her from pursuing her dream. Talk about rags to riches! Learn her wealth-building secrets and instantly 10X your prosperity and success.

Available in print and eBook from online retailers.

The Prosperous Author: Make a Living With Your Writing (Developing a Millionaire Mindset)

In Book One of *The Prosperity for Authors* series, *Developing a Millionaire Mindset*, you'll discover how to create the ultimate mindset for success. Master simple strategies to unlock your potential, overcome the fears that stop you from reaching your fullest potential, fight through your blocks, win your inner creative battles and develop unwavering resilient self-belief.

Although it was written for writers, the principles and strategies can be embraced by business entrepreneurs, actors, dancers, painters, photographers, filmmakers, and thousands of others around the world who want to enhance their mindset and elevate their success.

Available in print and eBook from online retailers.

The Prosperous Author: Productivity Hacks: Do Less & Make More

In Book Two of *The Prosperity for Authors series*, you'll learn how to work less and produce more, including powerhouse productivity tools you can harness to help you work smarter not harder, finish what you start, create new books and take them to market so you can sell them faster.

Although it was written for writers, the principles and strategies can be embraced by business entrepreneurs, actors, dancers, painters, photographers, filmmakers, and thousands of others around the world who want to enhance their mindset and elevate their success.

Available in print and eBook from online retailers.

The Prosperous Author-Two Book Bundle-Box Set (Books 1-2): Developing a Millionaire Mindset, Productivity Hacks: Do Less & Make More: How to Make a Living With Your Writing

Your blueprint for mastering a winning mindset, empowering purposeful productivity, making money and still having fun. By fuelling your desire, empowering your vision, slaying obstacles, mastering your subconscious mind, maintaining optimum health, empowering your relationships, and making a commitment to turn pro, you'll elevate your success.

Available in print and eBook from online retailers.

The Happy, Healthy Artist: Worry Less, Improve Your Health & Create a Sustainable Creative Career

Brimming with over 40 easy to apply strategies that will boost your mental, emotional and physical well-being, *The Happy, Healthy Artist* is a timeless call to action for anyone who wants to create a sustainable, joyful, writing and creative career.

Available in print and eBook from online retailers.

Stress Less. Love Life More: How to Stop Worrying, Reduce Anxiety, Eliminate Negative Thinking and Find Happiness

Are you feeling stressed, anxious, overwhelmed and just plain "over it"? Cassandra's newest release may provide the mojo boost you, or someone you love, need. Gain a fresh approach to living, from contemporary quick-fixes to help combat the pressures of modern day-to-day living, to soothing rituals and long-term solutions for a better life. This quintessential lifestyle guide reassures you that joy is within your reach, and shows you how to reclaim your, happiness, health, close relationships, career—and sanity.

Available in print and eBook from online retailers.

Financial Rescue: The Total Money Makeover: Create Wealth, Reduce Debt & Gain Freedom

You may not have the cash at the present moment, and the economy may not be ideal, but that doesn't mean your mind can't be working on your ideas and creating the way to a better future. *Financial Rescue* will show you how to reduce debt and create opportunities in every climate.

Available in print and eBook from online retailers.

Bounce: Overcoming Adversity, Building Resilience and Finding Joy

Bounce features the most essential and stirring passages from Gaisford's previous books, exploring topics such as meditation, mindfulness, positive health behaviors, and working with fear, depression, anxiety, and other painful emotions.

Bounce encourages a more playful approach to the seriousness of life and the ever-present stressors we all face. Through the course of this book, you will learn practical, creative and simple methods for heightening awareness and overcoming habitual patterns that block happiness and joy and hold you back.

Available in print and eBook from online retailers.

Bounce Companion Workbook

Hands on help to guide and support you **in practical, easy-to-understand steps.**

Bounce (the book) offers you information about overcoming adversity, building resilience and finding joy. Reading a book is great but applying the teachings and writing things down in a dedicated space helps bring the learning alive, deepens your self awareness, and enables you to make real world change. Reading gives you knowledge, but reflecting upon and applying that knowledge creates true empowerment.

The Bounce Companion Workbook will support you through the learning and show you how to create real and meaningful change in your life...simply and joyfully."

Mind Your Drink: The Surprising Joy of Sobriety. Control Alcohol and Love Life More: Discover Freedom, Find Happiness & Change Your Life

Anyone who needs to be kept on track or inspired to kick the drink habit and commit to living sober will find genuine help in this refreshingly insightful and solution-focused book.

Integrating neuroscience, cognitive therapy, proven tools, and teachings Cassandra blends Eastern and Western approaches to help people suffering from alcohol dependence and addiction.

"For readers who sincerely want to stop or rescue their drinking, but struggle to quit the drink habit, this book will pave the way."

Available in print and eBook from online retailers.

Mind Over Mojitos: How Moderating Your Drinking Can Change Your Life: Easy Alcohol-Free Recipes for Happier Hours & a Joy-Filled Life

Kick the alcohol habit. Join the trend toward mindful drinking. This delightful book is full of recipes for non-alcoholic drinks—perfect for anyone that might need to take a break from drinking and focus instead on reducing alcohol intake. Fun, simple and just what's needed for a creative break from drinking that can seriously change your life.

Available in print and eBook from online retailers.

Happy Sobriety: Alcohol and Guilt-Free Drinks You'll Love: Easy Recipes for Happier Hours & a Joy-Filled Life

Happy Sobriety brims with a range of a range of sexy, wonderfully refreshing and healthy alternatives to drinking alcohol.

Cut back or quit drinking entirely without becoming a hermit, being ostracized, or cutting back on an enjoyable social life. These easy to prepare drinks and pre-purchased alcohol-free alternatives can be enjoyed in the privacy of your own home, office party or hip location. "For readers who sincerely want to stop or rescue their drinking, but lack awareness of healthy alcohol-free alternatives, the recipes in this book will pave the way."

Available in print and eBook from online retailers.

The Sobriety Journal: The Easy Way to Stop Drinking: The Effortless Path to Being Happy, Healthy and Motivated Without Alcohol

This guided book leaves you free to create your own bespoke journal tailored to support your needs. Includes, Journal Writing Prompts, Empowering and Inspirational Quotes and Recovery Exercises that can be of use in your daily journal writing, working with your sponsor or use in a recovery group. The passion and purpose-inspired *Sobriety Journal* is the perfect place to begin your love affair. Think Brand New You!

Available in print and eBook from online retailers.

Change Your Mindset: Millionaire Mindset Makeover: The Power of Purpose, Passion, & Perseverance

Are you willing to face the biggest obstacle standing between you and success...the one between your ears?

Aided by scientifically proven research and practices, *Change Your Mindset* will help improve your thinking skills, win the battle over self-sabotaging thoughts, boost resilience and learn how to face and solve your problems in a constructive, liberating way. Discover the thinking flaws holding you back, empower your life with a prosperous mindset and change your life for the better. A complete and refreshing change of worldview is guaranteed after reading *Change Your Mindset—a* thought-provoking, science-backed, holistic guide.

Available in print and eBook from online retailers.

More of Cassandra's practical and inspiring workbooks on a range of career and life enhancing topics can be found on her Author Page and her website.

Newsletters

For inspiring tools and helpful tips subscribe to Cassandra's free newsletters here:

http://www.cassandragaisford.com

Sign up now and receive a free eBook!

COACHING AND WELLNESS THERAPIES

If you could free yourself from everything holding you back from living an incredible life —all of your fears, stinkin' thinking, limiting beliefs, negative emotions —you know you'd instantly feel happier, healthier and freer, right? But how? How can you liberate yourself from all that obstacles and blocks preventing you from living your best life?

The solution is so simple. Whether you have lost your job or hate the one you have, your relationship has hit a rough patch, or you're struggling with anxiety, depression, addiction or any other issues are impacting your life, talking to an impartial professional, qualified holistic therapist, counselor, and life coach can help.

I offer a range of transformational life and career rescue remedies, including:

• **Quantum Transformational Coaching** *(QTC)* to rapidly break-through limiting beliefs, sabotaging thoughts, subconscious blocks, and outdated scripts that are holding you back.

• **Akashic Records Soul Reading**—Unlock your destiny, heal the past, manifest a wonderful future. Achieve truly transformational and life-changing results fast.

• **Career Counselling** to help resolve career-related issues such as stress, role-conflict, job loss, workplace bullying, dissatisfaction, and assistance with career reinvention planning and self-employment coaching,

• **Personal therapy** provides early, solutions-focused intervention before problems escalate. A holistic approach to resolving many non-work issues including relationships, finances, physical and emotional well-being stress, grief, conflict, depression, lack of self-esteem, substance abuse...and more.

• **Life coaching** to help you when you don't need in-depth counseling. You may just be feeling stuck, lost, or demotivated, and need someone objective and supportive (and sometimes bossy!) to spur you on. Life coaching is solutions-focused, and rather than dwell on the past, focuses on where you are now, where you want to be and the steps and changes necessary to get you there

Live and work with purpose, passion, and prosperity no matter where you are in New Zealand or the world. I can help you reach your potential by phone, Skype or by e-mail. Schedule an appointment here—I'd love to provide guidance and support to help you live your best life.

Or, navigate to the following page to learn more about my wellness therapies and coaching services and how they can help you:

http://www.cassandragaisford.com/wellness-therapies/

> "Thank YOU! Our coaching was immensely helpful, and I have renewed hope for finding my way. You are simply lovely, and brilliant, and wise. So glad our energies aligned, and I found you! I am also so enjoying your books and will give more feedback as I go as well as post reviews online. And they will be GLOWING, I can assure you!"

~ Lisa Webb, artist

"A coaching session with Cassandra is like a light switch to a light bulb. My ideas were there but without that light switch I wasn't able to see them and manifest my dream of running a holistic business from home. Straight away, Cassandra was able to get to the heart of my core values and how to put them into a dream business. I now have the sense of purpose and drive to achieve my business goals. Cassandra's warm personality and positive approach make her a joy to work with. I recommend her to anyone who wants to unlock their personal and professional potential."

~ Shelley Sweeney, writer & Reiki practitioner

(Did you know that coaching fees are often tax deductible for people who use coaching to improve their professional skills? Check with your accountant for details.)

FOLLOW YOUR PASSION TO PROSPERITY ONLINE COURSE

If you need more help to find and live your life purpose you may prefer to take my online course, and watch inspirational and practical videos and other strategies to help you to fulfill your potential.

Follow your passion and purpose to prosperity—online coaching program

Easily discover your passion and purpose, overcoming barriers to success, and create a job or business you love with my self-paced online course.

Gain unlimited lifetime access to this course, for as long as you like—across any and all devices you own. Be supported with practical, inspirational, easy-to-access strategies to achieve your dreams.

To start achieving outstanding personal and professional results with absolute certainty and excitement. **Click here to enrol or find out more—the-coaching-lab.teachable.com/p/follow-your-passion-and-purpose-to-prosperity**

FURTHER RESOURCES

Documentaries and Movies

Making Good Men, Hollywood actor Manu Bennett (Azog the Defiler in the *Hobbit*) and former All Black Legend, Norm Hewitt share their personal stories of alcohol and how their lives and careers were nearly destroyed. A powerful story of tragedy, redemption, reconciliation and restoration. The documentary is no longer available on-demand, however if you would like to purchase a DVD copy email: fiona@teamokura.com.

http://www.teamokura.com/making-good-men/

The Truth About Alcohol, join British emergency room doctor Javid Abdelmoneim and other experts as they explore the benefits, risks and science of drinking. If you're determined to drink, you also discover ways to lessen the impact of alcohol.

https://www.netflix.com/nz/title/80185861

Support Groups

You'll find plenty of inspirational people who've devoted themselves to living joyfully alcohol-free. Here are just a few:

The Sobriety Experiment. Our dedicated Facebook community. We see a world where sobriety is normalized not stigmatized—you'll find plenty of support here.

https://www.facebook.com/Sobrietyexperiment

Hello Sunday Morning was founded in 2009 when Chris Raine undertook a year-long experiment to change his relationship with alcohol. A nightclub promoter at the time, Chris blogged about the challenges and successes of this experiment when he woke up hang-over-free. Join Chris and his movement towards a better drinking culture

https://www.hellosundaymorning.org/

No Beers, Who Cares encourages and supports a mindful approach to alcohol abstinence.

https://nobeerswhocares.com/pages/about

Sobriety Aotearoa proves support and fellowship to help you maintain sobriety

https://www.facebook.com/groups/sobrietyaotearoa/

Soberly Warrior. Founder Libby W. is passionate about encouraging women to have a positive and meaningful life that is not based around alcohol. You'll find plenty of encouragement here —https://www.facebook.com/soberlywarrior

Surf The Net

The New Zealand Health Promotions Agency provides an excellent guide to quickly gauge how much you're drinking—or intend to drink. The downloaded PDF can be found here —https://www.alcohol.org.nz/sites/default/files/images/1.0%20AL%20437%20Guide%20to%20Standard%20Drinks_FA_May2015_WEB.pdf

A good summary about the role of different parts of your brain and how alcohol affects optimal functioning can be found here —http://sciencenetlinks.com/student-teacher-sheets/alcohol-and-your-brain/.

Mathew Johnstone has a wide range of books and resources on mental wellness and mindfulness: www.matthewjohnstone.com.au

www.whatthebleep.com—a powerful and inspiring site emphasizing quantum physics and the transformational power of thought.

www.heartmath.org—comprehensive information and tools help you access your intuitive insight and heart-based knowledge. Validated and supported by science-based research. Check out the additional information about your heart-brain.

Experience the transformative power of hypnosis. One of my favorite hypnosis sites is the UK-based Uncommon Knowledge. On their website http://www.hypnosisdownloads.com you'll find a range of self-hypnosis mp3 audios to help you quit drinking.

Celebrity hypnotherapist and author Marissa Peer is another favorite source of subconscious reprogramming and liberation —www.marisapeer.com.

What beliefs are holding you back? Check out Peer's Youtube clip "How To Teach Your Mind That Everything Is Available To You" here —https://www.youtube.com/watch?v=IKeaAbM2kJg

Tim Ferriss recommends a couple of apps for those wanting some help getting started with meditation—Headspace (www.headspace.com) or Calm (www.calm.com).

National Geographic: The Science of Stress: Portrait of a killer

https://www.youtube.com/watch?v=ZyBsy5SQxqU

Effects of Stress on Your Body

https://www.youtube.com/watch?v=1p6EeYwp1O4

Mindfulness training

Wellington-based Peter Fernando offers an introductory guided meditation which you can take further. He also meets with individuals and groups in Wellington for philosophical talks on mindfulness and Buddhism. Very enjoyable and great for the soul.

http://www.monthofmindfulness.info

Guided meditations

www.calm.com

Free app with guided meditations

http://eocinstitute.org/meditation/emotional-benefits-of-meditation/

Includes a comprehensive list of the benefits of meditation.

Johann Hari, a long-time suffer of depression, says research into the medicalisation of trauma and mental health led him to unearth the liberating facts that he says drug companies conceal—learn more about how you can heal yourself and the great placebo cover-up. https://www.theguardian.com/media/2018/jan/07/johann-hari-depression-brain-lost-connections-book-interview

Books

Duff McKagan, the former bass guitarist of Guns N' Roses and one of the world's greatest rock musicians devised his own program of alcohol recovery. Read the inspiring story of a man who partied so hard he nearly died, *It's so Easy and Other Lies: Duff McKagan, The Autobiography.*

Russel Brand is a comedian and an addict. After being addicted to drugs, sex, fame, money and power, his book *Recovery: Freedom From Our Addictions* shares his journey, reinterprets The Twelve Step recovery process and champions the call for abstinence.

Drink: The Intimate Relationship Between Women and Alcohol—journalist and recovering alcoholic Anne Dowsett Johnson urges us all to wake up to the wilful blindness to the damages of drinking in our culture, and explores disturbing trends and false promises peddled by alcohol barons.

Fortify your superconscious power with Dr. Joe Dispenza— *Becoming Supernatural: How Common People Are Doing the Uncommon*

Power up with a new personality—read *Breaking the Habit of Being Yourself: How to Lose Your Mind and Create a New One* by Dr. Joe Dispenza.

Unleash the power of your mind by reading *You Are the Placebo: Making Your Mind Matter,* by Dr. Joe Dispenza.

How to Survive and Thrive in Any Life Crisis, Dr. Al Siebert

Thrive: The Third Metric to Redefining Success and Creating a Happier Life, Arianna Huffington

(This book has great content throughout and some excellent resources listed in the back.)

The Power of Now: A Guide to Spiritual Enlightenment, Eckhart Tolle

The Book of Joy, The Dalai Lama and Archbishop Desmond Tutu

The Sleep Revolution: Transforming Your Life One Night at a Time, Arianna Huffington

Quiet the Mind: An Illustrated Guide on How to Meditate, Mathew Johnstone

Comfortable with Uncertainty: 108 Teachings on Cultivating Fearlessness and Compassion, Pema Chodron

Power vs. Force: The Hidden Determinants of Human Behavior, David R. Hawkins

Learn how to live an inspired life with Tarot cards and other oracles. Read Jessa Crispin's book, *The Creative Tarot: A Modern Guide to an Inspired Life.*

Check out all of Collette-Baron-Reid's books, including: *Uncharted: The Journey Through Uncertainty to Infinite Possibility* and *Messages from Spirit: The Extraordinary Power of Oracles, Omens, and Signs.*

PLEASE LEAVE A REVIEW

Word of mouth is the most powerful marketing force in the universe. If you found this book useful, I'd appreciate you rating this book and leaving a review. You don't have to say much—just a few words about how the book helped you learn something new or made you feel.

"Your books are a fantastic resource and until now I never even thought to write a review. Going forward I will be reviewing more books. So many great ones out there and I want to support the amazing people that write them."

Great reviews help people find good books.

Thank you so much! I appreciate you!

PS: If you enjoyed this book, do me a small favour to help spread the word about it and share on Facebook, Twitter and other social networks.

ABOUT THE AUTHOR

Cassandra Gaisford, is a holistic therapist, award-winning artist, and #1 bestselling author. A corporate escapee, she now lives and works from her idyllic lifestyle property overlooking the Bay of Islands in New Zealand.

Cassandra is best known for the passionate call to redefine what it means to be successful in today's world.

She is a well-known expert in the area of success, passion, purpose and transformational business, career and life change, and is regularly sought after as a keynote speaker, and by media seeking an expert opinion on career and personal development issues.

Cassandra has also contributed to international publications and been interviewed on national radio and television in New Zealand and America.

She has a proven-track record of success helping people find savvy ways to boost their finances, change careers, build a business or become a solopreneur—on a shoestring.

Cassandra's unique blend of business experience and qualifications (BCA, Dip Pych.), creative skills, and well-ness and holistic training

(Dip Counselling, Reiki Master Teacher) blends pragmatism and commercial savvy with rare and unique insight and out-of-the-box-thinking for anyone wanting to achieve an extraordinary life.

Learn more about her on her website, her blog, or connect with her on Facebook and Twitter.

STAY IN TOUCH

FOLLOW ME AND CONTINUE TO BE INSPIRED

Follow Me And Continue To Be Supported, Encouraged, and Inspired

www.cassandragaisford.com
www.twitter.com/cassandraNZ
www.instagram.com/cassandragaisford
www.youtube.com/cassandragaisfordnz
www.pinterest.com/cassandraNZ
www.linkedin.com/in/cassandragaisford

BLOG

Be inspired by regular posts to help you increase your wellness, follow your bliss, slay self-doubt, and sustain healthy habits.

Learn more about how to achieve happiness and success at work and life by visiting my blog:

www.cassandragaisford.com/archives

SPEAKING EVENTS

Cassandra is available internationally for speaking events aimed at wellness strategies, motivation, inspiration and as a keynote speaker.

She has an enthusiastic, humorous and passionate style of delivery and is celebrated for her ability to motivate, inspire and enlighten.

For information navigate to
www.cassandragaisford.com/contact/speaking

To ask Cassandra to come and speak at your workplace or conference, contact: cassandra@cassandragaisford.com

NEWSLETTERS

For inspiring tools and helpful tips subscribe to Cassandra's free newsletters here:
http://www.cassandragaisford.com

Sign up now and receive a free eBook to help you find your passion and purpose!

COPYRIGHT

Cover by Cassandra Gaisford

Published by Blue Giraffe Publishing 2018

See our complete catalogue—www.cassandragaisford.com
ISBN eBook 978-0-9951080-6-6
ISBN print 978-0-9951080-7-3

First Edition

51604225R00119

Made in the USA
San Bernardino, CA
02 September 2019